The Spiritual Entrepreneur's ABC's

The Spiritual Entrepreneur's ABC's

To: Katie

The Righteous *and* Practical Guide to Business Success!

make it happen !
with Love

6/2020

Everett L. Courtney

The Spiritual Entrepreneur's ABC's

The Righteous *and* Practical Guide to Business Success!

Everett L. Courtney

Veronica Lane Books

 Veronica Lane Books
Books That Make a Difference!

2554 Lincoln Blvd Ste. 142, Los Angeles, CA 90291 USA
Tel: +1(833) VLBOOKS +1(833-852-6657)
www.VeronicaLaneBooks.com

ISBN 978-1-7341800-4-6

Library of Congress Cataloging-In-Publication Data /Pending

DEDICATION

To Everett Louis Courtney, Jr., who perished in a senseless act of greed and stupidity. My son, I am forever grateful that you came into my life, giving me a sense of drive and purpose. When you arrived here on Planet Earth on October 7, 1980, I was filled and thrilled with a joy that I never felt before that day. Thank you for all the lessons that you have given me related to fatherhood, manhood, and most of all, brotherhood. Continue to rest in the peaceful realm of the spirit.

Love you always,
Dad

ACKNOWLEDGMENTS

I am deeply grateful to have an array of beautiful people who have helped me to become the shining light that I never knew I could be someday. All these prescient people saw the light in me when I could only see the darkness. My whole life has been, and continues to be, one of unfolding, aided by my friends, mentors, and guides. This God-sent team effort has allowed me to have a life truly worth living.

I extend my deepest gratitude to all the players in my life who guided and assisted me in my endeavors as an entrepreneur. I thank my mother, Eddie Jean Courtney, who laid the groundwork. I thank all of those who mentored me in my formative years, including the late Dr. John Rossi, who saw that spark of ambition in me when I first met him at the tender age of ten. Dr. Rossi introduced me into a world of very successful business people, who I had no idea even existed. I thank my God-Mom, Alice Jenkins, who is still today a major factor in my life and success.

I am grateful to have been mentored by the late Bishop Tommie Lawrence and his wife, Charlesetta Lawrence, along with John Littlejohn, William Campbell, Jimmy and Joy Moore, Sydney and Charles Zerah, Muhammad Nasserdine, Jewel Thais Williams, and Carol Williams, and my godparents Pastor Willie Cockroft and Dr. Jini Kilgore Cockroft.

I also want to thank Rev. Ike, Rev. Candice Gee, Rev. Susan Shahani, Rev. Leon Campbell, Rev. Cheryl Ward, Rev. Coco Stewart, Greta Sesheta, George Thompson, my financial advisor and Dr. Cheyenne Bryant, my life coach; also, Rev. Dr. Michael Beckwith, Dr. Rickie Byers, Dr. John Goff, Akili Beckwith, Les Brown, Lisa Nichols, T. Harv Eckhart, V. Hansen, George Frazier, Earl Graves, Robert Allen, Bill Marriot, Warren Buffet, and President Barack Obama.

This book is an acknowledgement of my gratitude to all the new thought and ancient wisdom teachers and students throughout the world; too numerous to name, that includes the entire Agape Community and practitioners, my God's House of Prayer for All Nations community, my high school sweetheart Trace Fisher, and all of my friends, brothers and sisters, and children. All of you have been inspirational! Peace and richest blessings to all of you for the inspiration, motivation, and dedication you instilled in me.

INTRODUCTION

Dear Reader,

    I am very glad that I am able to share these golden nuggets of experience-based wisdom with you. Many of the truths found here were learned through trial and error. I was a no matter what type of entrepreneur, meaning that if I felt a need to do something, I just did it. I rarely researched anything, Instead, most of the time I just took action and somehow I knew I would be all right. However, I did come across some major challenges in doing things this way. I now know that if I can garner the experience of someone who has been down the road before me, I can gain valuable insight. Therefore, this book is designed to give you the insights that I know will assist you in being a successful and prosperous entrepreneur.

    One thing is for sure: Universal law and principles are the same for everyone, so everybody can use them even at an early age. Hence, the book certainly is an ABCs of Entrepreneurs that can be useful to anyone at any age. I started my first successful business at the age of six as a shoe shine boy. I parlayed that into a profitable paper route, all before I was nine years old. I later started another service business mowing lawns in my community, which led me into the jewelry business selling hand-to-hand to members of my community and church. I have had business successes, ranging from manufacturing to wholesale trade to real estate, to my work now as an author and speaker.

    From selling jewelry, I went to selling sold marijuana but when I got busted, I took the proceeds from the drug business and opened a jewelry store in downtown Los Angeles. There I manufactured and designed rings, chains, watches, pendants, bracelets, and other types of jewelry, which I sold wholesale. I was able to build up a national distribution, and later opened another retail/wholesale location in the San Diego area.

    Business was booming for me from the 80's until the late 90's, when I decided to open a night club and restaurant, which also included a prostitution, gambling, and drug den. From a monetary standpoint, I was very successful but I was unfulfilled. I eventually sold my stake in this business to my partner, the late Dickie McKnight. McKnight was a very flamboyant night club owner who was killed after being ambushed and robbed while sitting in his Phantom Rolls Royce in front of his Baldwin Hills, California, home.

    At about this time, I was hedging my bets by investing heavily in the real estate and stock markets. I bought properties in California, Arizona,

Illinois, Florida, and Nevada, to name a few, but I didn't know anything about being a developer. This was just another adventure for me, so I jumped in full throttle, only to lose my pants, shirt, and tie when I went bankrupt due to the recession that hit us in 2008. LOL! So, please trust the principles in this writing to be tried and true because I got all of my education at RWU, Real World University!

To Your Success, Always!
Everett L. Courtney

A

Age

Four Years Old, Going on Five!

I can say for sure that I became an entrepreneur at a very early age. I believe that I was able to achieve and ignite my gift of asking because it was God-given and embedded within me. I believe that just as an acorn knows that it is coded to be an oak tree, I was coded to be an entrepreneur.

I was only four years old when I asked some ladies walking down the street if they wanted to buy some pies. They inquired, "What kind of pies do you have?" Because I was outside playing in the dirt, I responded, "Mud pies." I made the dirt stick together by putting it in a cup which served as a mold for the pies. Then I emptied each pie out of the cup and stacked it neatly side-by-side with the other pies.

When the ladies asked me, "How much?" I answered, "A quarter," and I made fifty cents that fast. This was around 1968 in Chicago, my hometown.

Remember that God does not know age, gender, finances. You are never too young to start your entrepreneurial career. I was certainly mature beyond my age but that maturity can start early on in life, especially once an individual identifies their real needs beyond the childish ones.

Awake

The Power of Asking!

That fifty cents brought me into a keen awakened state that, from that day to this one, I can recall so vividly how I crafted, manufactured, and sold those mud pies. The spark from that sale helped me wake up early on to learn to ask what I wanted.

I was so happy to get that fifty cents that I took my sister and myself to the store, and we bought several pieces of our favorite candy, along with a soda pop.

From then on, every time I played outside, whether snow was falling or the sun was shining, I made something to ask people to buy—and I always made a sale!

This was the very beginning of my salesmanship ability. I was awake to a power within me. I was never afraid to ask someone to buy from me. I had woken up to the power of asking for something. Some people ignored me; however, most gave me a smile or bought something.

If you don't ask, you don't get. Be sure you are asking for the right thing. And learn how to ask in a way that you won't get No! for an answer. Get awake to the innate power of asking for what you want, and remove any self-doubt or hindrances that get in the way of that power.

Always

There is Always an Opportunity!

I didn't know at that early age that one day I would become an amazing salesman. From those initial street sales, I discovered another business. While walking around the neighborhood, I would see bottles on the back of people's porches, so I began to knock on my neighbors' doors and ask if I could have the bottles. Most of them replied, "Sure, you can have them." Some people asked me what I was going to do with them, and I answered, "Take them back to the store and redeem them for a nickel."

Every day I found a new neighbor who would give me some bottles, and I surely took them to the store to redeem them for money. After a little while, I had to make more than one trip. With my energy and my budding skills, I was always looking for more sales opportunities. In fact, I built up a little early recycling business!

An entrepreneur is always on the lookout for opportunities. There are endless signs that the Universe presents to you if you are always awake and ready to act on a moment's notice. Always keep all your senses alert and your mind sharp. And incidentally, that means that you should always keep away from substances that do the opposite to your physical and mental capacities. To a serious and ambitious entrepreneur, always means always!

Action

Take Action!

Taking action by asking for what I wanted helped to wake me up to a very important aspect of entrepreneurship. I learned easily that if I wanted something, I had to do something. And boy, was I willing to do not just something, but almost anything!

I got so excited when I saw an opportunity to make some cash, it became natural to me to take action. I was never really afraid of taking action even though there were some folks who would shout at me and say, "No, boy. Go home." But I would shrug it off. It was comical for me to see people act rude or immature to a young man with entrepreneurial energy.

Instead of allowing their behavior to get to me, I had many days when I actually laughed at these types of shortsighted people. God knows that this attitude has surely served me well over the years. Any entrepreneur will get a lot of rejection in the form of straight ahead No! However, now that I am older and more experienced, I know that an affirmative Yes! can be right behind that initial rejection once you learn the art of overcoming obstacles by taking actions that move you over, around or even under those obstacles.

Remember that actions come in 3 forms: mental, verbal and physical. As an entrepreneur learn how to coordinate and time your actions for the best results. Before you take a verbal or physical action, wouldn't it be wise to engage first in a mental action?

Everybody is familiar with Newton's law that every action has an equal and opposite reaction. Learn to know the consequences of your actions, preferably before you take action. Every attorney asking a witness questions frames their questions to get exactly the answer they want from the witness. An entrepreneur's actions must be well-planned too. Act wisely!

Available

Always Be Available!

Making myself available was another critical aspect to my becoming an entrepreneur. I began to know most of my neighbors and they began to know me as an energetic and multi-talented young man willing to try almost anything. Soon they started to call on me to do odd jobs for them.

As one door opened, another one closed, and vice versa. Example: In the summer, I would water my neighbors' lawns and in the winter, I would shovel their snow. When one seasonal job ends, another one opens! Get it? I also would help my neighbors carry groceries home in my used little red wagon that I got from my Mama as a Christmas gift from the Salvation Army.

Making myself available to my neighbors led me to observe other opportunities to expand the small empire I was continuously building for myself. I often made store runs for the elderly people in the neighborhood, which always came with a quarter or fifty-cent tip. Actually, there were more opportunities than I had time for, considering school and homework!

Being available means that you, as an entrepreneur, are always available in body, mind and spirit. There are literally signs everywhere that the Universe puts out for you if you are available mindfully in the moment. If you are available in your meditation practice, the Universe will speak to you and you will hear the message. Your business (and personal) guidance can come from any direction—from a child, a song on your car radio, an advertisement, anything external or internal—if you just remain available.

Assistance

Being of Assistance is a Blessing!

I truly feel that I became so blessed as an entrepreneur simply because I was always willing to give and share my earnings first with my mother, and then with my siblings and friends. I quickly became known as the 'Candy Man' because I always brought candy around for my friends and family.

I would be so happy when my mom would count my money and then smile proudly at me. During that time, my mom was single and unemployed with six kids. She didn't qualify for public assistance because, though separated from her husband, her divorce was not yet final. Therefore, she needed all the help she could get to keep food on the table, to keep the lights and gas on, and to keep the rent paid.

Making money was fun for me but knowing that I was able to help use that money where it was needed was more important. This is an early lesson that I have carried with me through all my entrepreneurial endeavors.

Learn that your entrepreneurial venture should be of assistance, not just to yourself, but also to your employees, your clients, your family and friends, and your community. If you are only motivated by selfish needs and aspirations, of course you can succeed. But as the Bible reminds us, "God loves a cheerful giver." Be of assistance through your business and you will certainly get a lot more support from the Universe. And be cheerful about your assistance.

Aware

Be Aware of Your World!

Soon I actually became aware of who had money and who didn't have it. Something in me allowed me to look at a person and discern if he or she had money or not. I learned early that most of the very flashy people that I encountered on the streets of Chicago did have money. I would look at how people were dressed, what vehicle they were riding in, and whether they were wearing jewelry, among other indicators. Often, my assessment was accurate.

With this awareness, I became buddy-buddy with all of the neighborhood working girls, dealers, pimps, players, as well as legitimate business owners. I never judged any of them. They all played a very prominent role in my future development and my keen awareness of people. I could size a person up at the drop of a dime, and this really benefitted me in my entrepreneurial endeavors.

Being aware as an entrepreneur, as I have discussed also in Awake, means that you not only become more and more keenly aware of your surroundings and the people coming and going in and out of your life. Being aware, means also that you learn about and align yourself with the laws of the Universe. There are moral and ethical laws to become aware of, and you must remain aware of when you are straying from those laws. I recommend you find not only a business mentor but a spiritual teacher who can guide you toward the deepest truths by which every truly happy and successful entrepreneur abides by and uses for the benefit of his entrepreneurial venture as well as the good of all those souls who surround them. Be constantly aware of these truths!

Advice

Listen to Those with More Experience!

My skills of awareness deepened and helped me maneuver away from individuals that might want to do me harm. However, I could not avoid encountering several of the neighborhood bullies who saw me making money and who, when they caught me by myself, would either snatch my money away or extort it from me by threatening to beat me up if I didn't give it to them.

When I told my mom about it, she said, "Boy, hide your dollars in your shoes or socks, but keep a small amount of change in your pocket, so when the bullies come you tell them you will give them half the change if they will walk you home." This is how I avoided getting my little behind kicked most of the time.

Eventually, I turned my bullies into my friends by sharing my money with them, and I now had friends and protection from most of the other neighborhood bullies. This one piece of advice from my mom helped me survive and thrive in the street environment of my childhood.

Know where you are getting advice from on your entrepreneurial journey. Learn to value good advice. And most importantly, learn to follow good advice promptly and thoroughly!

Advantage

Take Advantage Every Day!

As you can tell now from my story by now, I had very little advantage in the common usage of the word. I was certainly born and raised in what is called a 'disadvantageous environment.' The definition of advantage is 'involved in or creating favorable circumstances that increase the chances of success or effectiveness; beneficial.' But I learned how to gain an advantage very early in life.

I always found a way to earn money. I know now that I was anointed to do what I do because I did it so effortlessly. Maybe that is my advantage, some sort of natural outgoing and selling personality. I could come out of the house any day of the week and know for sure that somehow I was going to create an opportunity to make some money that day.

I was, and I am today, always seeking ways to make things advantageous for my family and me. I took advantage of the seasons: winter, summer, spring, and fall. I always found a way to create an opportunity to make money. If I saw someone else doing something that I thought I could do to make some money, I took advantage of that inspiration that the Universe had provided for me.

Each season brought out a different advantage for me, and I never even thought about not having advantages. I guess that's the beauty of being a kid and not knowing any better but somehow realizing innately where the advantages are, especially those that are right in front of you.

As an entrepreneur, I suggest you create a list of your perceived advantages and disadvantages. The advantages you possess, seek ways to expand and capitalize on those. The disadvantages you perceive, seek ways to turn those around into advantages. Be honest and then get to work based on this kind of self-evaluation.

Abundance

Appreciate Abundance!

I never heard the word "abundance" as a kid. Instead, I saw a lot of despair, hopelessness, poverty, drugs, addiction and junkies line the streets of the Chicago ghettoes where I grew up. At one point, I met a pimp named Flukey who put me in his brand new Cadillac Eldorado one day and we drove downtown to the Loop to have lunch. This was a real eye opener for me.

I saw white businessmen coming and going into an absolutely gorgeous restaurant—a place I did not know existed—with white linen covered tables, white linen napkins, and man waitresses and waiters in black suits busily serving the diners. I had never seen or dreamed of anything like this before.

When I later found out how to get back to this restaurant, my world of abundance came into being because I saw the opportunity to start my third business: a shoe shine stand. Boy! I would ask for a quarter a shine, and sometimes get a dollar and sometimes even five dollars, along with a really fancy meal. I was truly living the life of abundance at the ripe young age of six! I understood and appreciated the abundance of life early on and I made it my goal to always be part of that abundance.

As entrepreneur, of course we value material abundance but ask yourself where that abundance originates from at the start. If you go out to nature, you really understand abundance more graphically. The Universe is infinitely abundant. There is no limit to Source because that is what it is—the Source of everything! Learn to align yourself in business and personally with the endlessly abundant Source that is all around us and is always ready to enhance itself through our pure intentions and efforts. Understand and align yourself with the universal laws of abundance at the deepest levels and many doors of opportunity will open to you. And don't forget to share your abundance!

B

Birthright

Our Precious Gifts!

As a young boy, I never understood exactly what it meant to have a birthright. I now know that each person has the right by birth to unfold to his or her greatness. We all are endowed with natural gifts and talents with which I believe we come to this physical plane called life.

One of the many good things about being here in the land known as America is that we can develop our gifts and then expand on what we have brought to this existence through capitalism. We can monetize our gifts as we share them with the world. Whatever you came here to release, I say be open and honest with yourself and pursue it with relentless passion, and I can guarantee that you will be successful in your endeavors.

Our birthright demands our passion, which is the stuff that breeds successful people. Our birthright demands that we be brave, meaning that we are not afraid to act courageously. The Buddha said, "A human birth is a most precious thing." Every minute deserves our full gratitude, appreciation and thanksgiving for being given a human birth. It is our birthright and our duty to fulfill the best destiny we can by being a beneficial presence on the planet, particularly through our own personal development and by our labors or business offerings.

Bold

Be Bold, In Spite of Fears!

In Psalm 100 you will find the passage, "Make a joyful noise to the Lord, all the earth." To make a joyful noise is a bold gesture, isn't it? I interpret that to mean, proclaim boldly and in a thankful manner all that you have been given materially and spiritually.

As an entrepreneur take charge of your gifts and talents, and trust in them for they are the seeds of what you can achieve in this life. Find the right soil and conditions so that when the opportune season arrives your inherited seeds will boldly grow and flourish. A mighty oak tree boldly rose from an acorn seed. Each of us started from an invisible genetic origin and each of us can rise to our fullest and unlimited potential. These are bold facts, aren't they?

Being an entrepreneur is not for wimps. You have to overcome your own fears plus the fears that have been ingrained in us by our parents, school, church and media. Boldness is a fundamental quality in becoming a successful entrepreneur. It takes bold and brave steps to mount a successful campaign in which each move is calculated and audaciously pursued. Being bold means being confident, self-assured, nervy, valiant and even impudent and brash. Use your brains, get advice and support and then boldly march forward to your destiny of success. Drive yourself to the place you want to go by being bold!

Boy

An Entrepreneur in a Boy's Body!

My boyhood, I tell you, held some of the best and worst times of my life. I am so very glad that as a boy I didn't harbor resentment towards people for what they did or didn't do for me.

I never knew who my biological father was until I was well over twenty-one years of age. I met him in a casket with his lifeless body being honored just before he was buried. I didn't really know the circumstances of what happened between him and my mother but I never felt any resentment toward this man that I never knew.

I learned early on that when you have a goal or a mission that you want to accomplish as an entrepreneur, you have to accept your early childhood life experiences and learn from them. Starting as a boy (or a girl) the child has to learn to continue moving beyond boundaries, rules, regulations, naysayers, negativity, situations and circumstances. Being a boy-child taught me this very early in life.

As you move through life you will notice boys that are in men's bodies. Some men never grow up emotionally beyond being 10 or 12 years old. There are girls in women's bodies also. Look carefully at the people you encounter in life and business. Are you dealing with a juvenile or an adult? And which are you?

And don't forget when you meet a real young boy (or a young girl) that you are possibly meeting a potentially great future leader, businessperson, surgeon or scientist. You should be motivated to offer that young person some encouragement on their own life or entrepreneurial path.

Best

Know You Have Done Your Best!

What truly served me and helped me to become an entrepreneur was always maintaining my ideal to do my best in each area of my endeavors. As a shoe shine boy, I always was thinking about how I could make a shoe shine and sparkle like a star. As a paper boy, I always wanted my paper to be delivered on time and in the best condition possible. Each endeavor for me was always about being considerate and on time.

Much of my success came not just from maintaining my ideals but by actually doing my best despite any obstacle that came my way. I had no formal training but my personal values and my follow-through made me bold enough to jump into something and learn along the way the best I could. Of course, I often messed up but my sincerity, my consideration of others plus my desire to be and do my best, accelerated my entrepreneurial successes and my overall feeling that at the end of the day I had done my best.

Notice that I did not say, "I will try to do my best." That kind of statement is not bold and allows neuro-linguistically for an out, an excuse. Always say, "I do my best!" Understanding the neuroscience that how we phrase our lives mentally and verbally very much determines the outcome of our efforts. In Japanese, they don't have the expression, "Good Luck!" Instead, they say "Gambate!" meaning, "Do your best!" You know you are doing your best when the best outcome arrives. Do your best!

Believe

You Gotta Believe It!

One thing I can say for sure is that belief in your dreams and aspirations is the fuel that can sustain you over the long haul. I believed in my ability to sell so much that I felt as though no matter what the product or service was, I would ultimately be successful if I truly believed that I would be.

As an entrepreneur, understand that belief is a very strong force in the Universe. Anyone who has done or is doing great things in this life absolutely has to believe that they can do it. Henry Ford famously said, "If you believe you can, or you believe you can't, you're right!"

Maybe you need a coach, a teacher, or a parent to teach you to believe in yourself, but please trust me that nothing great has ever been accomplished by people who didn't believe that it was possible.

In medicine, it has been proved over and over again that a placebo can have the same effect as a real medicine given to a patient. The power of belief creates realities. Another easy way to understand it: Fake it till you make it! That is, you can pretend strongly enough through your belief in yourself or your product or service that you can achieve the success you know is imminent.

Make your entrepreneurial story another example of a person who did great things because of their strong belief that they could do anything they formulated in their mind and heart.

Better

Better is Better!

As an entrepreneur, understand that you must strive to be better than you were yesterday or the day before, or the year before. Of course you need to be better than your competition but that can only happen as you get smarter personally and in your entrepreneurial efforts. I am not saying you have to be a better person than anyone else, in a comparative way because in God's eyes we are all equal.

However, you want to continue to get better and better, for example at your skill sets, such as getting more inside info on your industry sector. You want to learn to how to improve your product or service, how to better deliver your commercial offerings, how to better present your sales pitch, and how to better your leadership abilities.

New technology displaces the old, and in come new and better ways than when you first started your entrepreneurial venture. Better continues to do better, and to get better every entrepreneur must understand this very basic concept. Time brings about change; everything under the sun changes, and change is inevitable. So, as an entrepreneur, be mindful that you are always changing for the better through better thinking and action.

Start as early as possible to develop a process to garner the insights that help you to perform better and succeed better. Use your meditation practice, guidance from your mentors, input from your team, and your research—anything that helps you do better. The urge to do better absolutely will result in more and more positive outcomes.

Bright

Always Be Bright!

As an entrepreneur, it is mandatory to look on the bright side of your situation. There will be times when business will be slow, employees will mess up, people will disappoint you, the government will unfairly tax you, and just about everything undesirable that can happen will happen.

If you are not looking on the bright side, then people, circumstances and situations will wear you down. Remember, the glass is always half full. Tomorrow's weather will be partly sunny, not partly cloudy. This neuro-linguistic understanding of language, as previously mentioned, is very important to keeping a bright perspective. For example, I never use the word 'hope' as in, "I hope you feel better tomorrow." Instead I say, "I know you will feel better tomorrow!" Hear the difference?

It is important during dark days to remember that you are giving and sharing your gifts and talents, and to remember that this is why you do what you do in the first place. Life has so many challenges with negative talk, with fear and doubt, and with what appear to be unfortunate incidents. Are you going to curtail your ultimate success by allowing the passing shadow to stop you? Wake up every day on the best side of life—which is the bright side of life!

C

Create

You Are a Creator!

As entrepreneurs, we must first understand our ability to create opportunities for ourselves, and for the products and services that can benefit others. This is because we all come here with the ability to create things. In fact, it is our Divine assignment to create things for the benefit of humanity, whether for profit or non-profit causes.

Therefore, I say that if you can dream up a plan for your life, I suggest that you create a vision for what you expect of your life and from your life. Life will give you that which you are willing to create with your conscious and subconscious mind. How far can you extend your creative abilities? Is there a limit to your abilities to create?

As you hold onto that which you want to create, in due season the subconscious mind will connect with the Superconscious mind. Once you are aligned with the Creator in your wholesome thoughts, words and deeds, you will feel the infinite power of Creation pulling you along to your biggest and best vision. You will begin to see and experience your creation in ways that unfold beyond your wildest imagination. Always be in the creative mode so that more and more doors of opportunity are opened for you.

Care

Truly Care for Yourself!

Understanding the importance of care is vitally important for an entrepreneur. First, there is self-care. Learn as quickly as possible to take care of the most vital aspects of your being. This entails care for your mind, body, and soul.

To take care of your mind, I suggest spending time daily in the stillness of your being. I like meditation. Maybe you like listening to music or the stillness of a silent night but take that time to reflect on where you are and where you want to go. It also is very important to care for your body by eating nutritious food and exercising. I like to eat fresh, organic fruits and vegetables. For exercise, I enjoy yoga, walking, bike riding, and swimming.

On your spiritual side, it is important to know, connect and care about the spirit guide that always resides within you. That guide comes in the form of a clear voice and will care for you. You will hear and know how to steer in the right direction with clues about the things that concern you through your both your business and personal quests. An absolute knowing is possible when you care to be aligned with your intuition, for intuition is one way your spirit guide guides you.

If you care for yourself in these ways, your capacities as an entrepreneur will only become more enhanced, your success will certainly be more assured.

Conquest

Conquering Demons!

Conquest is the overcoming of a problem or weakness. We all will encounter some form of problem if we are living here on Planet Earth. However, we did not come to this plane to be a crazy conquer like a Genghis Khan or Hernan Cortez. As an entrepreneur, you are facing both internal and external challenges throughout your career. The inner conquest—ridding yourself of unwholesome thoughts, words and deeds—this is the basic place to start your conquest.

As you are consciously and mindfully working to conquer any inner challenges or obstacles, you are simultaneously working to conquer the everyday challenges and obstacles that come up in your business life. The sooner you can realize your problem and work to conquer it by finding a strong opposing force to obliterate it, the quicker you will become a successful entrepreneur, even a conquistador!

A successful entrepreneur is a great problem solver, and they have the ability to overcome any weakness by getting the appropriate help. I had to conquer a multitude of personal problems in my life. Yes, I have been addicted to just about everything that isn't good for anyone: alcohol, drugs, food, gambling, sex, and work. I had to work hard to conquer these self-sabotaging obstacles within me, to do the painful inner work as well to persistently develop solid healthy habits.

At some critical point in your life, you have to make adult choices and decisions in order to conquer the demons within you that that stand in the way of your life's purpose and progress. Then, and only then, will you have the power to become a true conqueror in business!

Conversation

Learn the Art of Conversation!

An entrepreneur learns how to converse with the various people that you are going to meet so that you can do business with them. In addition to foreign-language speakers, specialty groups have their own particular lingo or trade language. For example, medical doctors use medical terms; lawyers, legal terms; accountants, financial terms; and so on with politicians, police officers, singers, writers, bankers, loan officers, and investors. Learn to be conversant in as many areas as possible within your industry sector and in any other sectors that interest you.

At some point in your journey, you are going to converse with people from different parts of the world as you expand your business globally. You will find that the more you are able to communicate with your foreign contacts in their language—even just using a few key foreign expressions or learning some of the technical jargon that various professionals use in their sector— the more successful you will be as an entrepreneur.

I lived in California and Florida, both of which have large Hispanic populations. When I taught myself how to speak Spanish, my sales improved. Spanish-speaking people felt comfortable doing business with me. Today, I can converse fluently in many languages; including financial and banking, real estate and legal, literature and music, geopolitical and yes, even in the true language of love. Converse, communicate and prosper!

Communication

Good Communications, Good Business!

Communication is much different than conversation. Think about how many people speak English together and still miscommunicate. A truly successful entrepreneur learns early on that communication is really more about listening, than speaking. Maybe you heard as a child, "When you're talking, you're not listening. When you're not listening, you're not learning." The same maxim is even truer in business, especially in negotiation.

The faster you can understand and harness the importance of real communication, the faster you will be able to accelerate the success of your business venture. Many entrepreneurs are fast and smooth talkers but I have found few who understand the art of communication through listening. When I ask the right question and listen intently for the answer, I hear what my customer wants and needs for our deal to succeed. This art of listening is what keeps a business thriving; listening and hearing carefully to the client in order to target exactly what they want from your product or service.

The client always, and I mean always, will let you know exactly what you need to know if you learn the basic principles of communication. There are many, many books written on building both business and personal communication skills. We can't get into the subject as deeply as it needs to be understood in this book. Do the research and read some of those books as soon as possible. There is even an entire science called Neuro Linguistic Programming (NLP) that teaches which single words to use and not use in order to engender ultimate achievements through successful communications.

We see what kind of harm not communicating properly can do in our personal lives, even globally. Lots of businesses and business people have gone under simply because they did not hear what the customer wanted, and they responded in inappropriate ways. Understand communication!

Confidence

Not the False Kind!

Having supreme confidence in your abilities, your product or service is not being arrogant or over-zealous. Call it a certainty base on realistic evaluations. You know that you have developed your skills, knowledge, and your capacities to truly deliver on your promise.

Oftentimes, inexperienced entrepreneurs have a good product and service but they portray a lack confidence in their abilities. Investors, bankers, and buyers pick up very fast on even on the slightest self-doubt. Remember that your backers or experienced buyers are in a sense entrepreneurs themselves, and they have to rely on their very basic instincts to determine trust and commitment, even with the brilliant 50 page business plan you have put in front of them.

Therefore, go about your business with confidence, meaning that you are simply being truthful about what you can and cannot deliver. You prove to yourself and your customers that you can deliver what you promised in a timely fashion. The more proof of your competence, the more your confidence grows.

However, remember that I am not talking about false confidence or bravado. Be confident of and true to your code of conduct, as well as realistic with the goods in inventory or the services you can deliver. Your client's trust and confidence in you will grow exponentially. Your proven confidence may even put a little swagger in walk!

Confidant

Someone with Who You Can Really Talk!

Entrepreneurs need confidants. A confidant is defined as a person with whom one shares a secret or private matter, trusting them not to repeat it to others. Find and keep one or two persons in your circle to whom you can confide your innermost thoughts and feelings about your business, and even your personal side. There are going to be times when you hit a roadblock. At such times, not having the right team member to confide in can cause you to stumble and fall. Without having the right person to help steer you back on the right track, you may experience confusion, anxieties or delays.

Business is not always a linear affair, meaning that random and chance events may occur that throw your plans off track. Sometimes your own missteps come back to haunt you in the form of penalties and bad faith. You may need to confide in someone to get solace or advice.

Your confidant can be part of your team such as your attorney, accountant, VP, or an outside consultant, depending upon how big your operation is. You might even see the benefit of having a board of directors that you can confide in, especially if they have lots more business experience than you.

Even if you are just starting out on the entrepreneur's journey, find a wise and experienced family member who has a successful business and who can provide expertise and guidance. Having a business confidant definitely accelerate your business growth.

Co-Play

Work as Play!

It is very effective if your entrepreneurial enterprise is formed in such a way that the owner and team players feel that they have come together to play for the common good of the business and its customers. Any business venture should be fun and enjoyable. Neuroscience has shown that people are 30% smarter when they are smiling, open and feeling safe.

From the time you start up until the time and as long as your business flourishes, you should be so exhilarated that you can't wait to go to work every day. You are having fun and that is what this whole entrepreneur lifestyle is about. It's about being in total alignment with your gifts, talents, and purpose on this planet. Work hard, play hard—all together!

Let the team act, sing, dance, play sports, and do a host of other fun and bonding activities together, even during the business day. It is vitally important that all of what you and your company are doing becomes a co-play. Of course, you put a lot of serious thought, effort and money into your venture but there also has to be a sense of gamesmanship, comradery and fun involved too. You are playing seriously in order to co-create a product or service for the benefit of humanity too. Once you develop a mindset of co-play, your harvest will be a in the form of a well-deserved and lucrative co-payments.

Control

Learn Self-Control First!

If you can't control yourself, you cannot control others. As an entrepreneur see yourself also being a valuable steward of life. That means that you are in control of the welfare of other people, including your team, your family and friends and your community.

Learn to control yourself and you will be much more able to effectively control your organization. I have hurt myself and others by not monitoring or controlling my emotions, through reckless spending and needless over-indulgences. You must relentlessly work to control your thoughts, actions, and deeds.

Many people have had tremendous gifts and talents, along with resources that they bring to their entrepreneurial venture. However, if an individual has no effective control of their impulses, desires, emotions, attitudes, and words, they will eventually fail. If self-control is absent, an individual easily lands himself or herself in situations from which they may not be able to escape.

Just look at the number of singers, athletes, business people, and other professionals that have crumbled to dust due to inadequate or ineffective control of themselves. Study your habitual behaviors, where you act impulsively or rudely, where you take offense, or not being wholly mindful of the moment. Reflect on the qualities that impede your progress as an entrepreneur due to lack of self-control.

Then start to vision the positive qualities that you want to cultivate and seek the methods toward positive change. I have found over the years that it's when I am in control of my thoughts, speech and actions that I always do my best as an entrepreneur, and as an ordinary person.

D

Decide

Time to Step Up!

An entrepreneur must know how, when, and what to decide. On a personal level, decide how many hours a day you want to work. Decide if you are going to work on weekends and holidays. Decide if your religious preference forbids you to work on certain days, and if you will honor your religion's teachings. Decide what's best for your family, co-workers, team members, or associates.

Decision-making is a very critical factor in any business. Having the ability to make quick and firm decisions will definitely help to accelerate your business growth or start-up. As you launch out to be a successful entrepreneur, take into account that you now become "The Decider," in the famous word coinage of George W. Bush. Another famous quote is, "The Buck Stops Here." You, as the fearless leader of your entrepreneurial venture, must make hard decisions about finances, business strategies, your employees and your business partners.

Taking time out of your business, personal or social life is very important in order to step back in order to become a powerful decision-maker. You must see as many perspectives and consequences of where your decision will take you in your business, personally and even socially. You can always reach out to a partner, confidant or mentor to discuss an important business matter but ultimately you will bear the responsibility of making the decision. Decide now that you can do this!

Degrees

Do You Have to Have One?

Having an academic degree in a specific area of endeavor is not always necessary. We know of many very successful men and women who launched out into the deep waters of entrepreneurship without any formal education or just partial education. You'd be surprised how many billionaires don't have a college degree; individuals such as Bill Gates, Mark Zuckerberg and David Geffen were all dropouts!

I personally never finished my formal education but as an entrepreneur I have earned (and lost) millions. I am a huge fan of education, especially if you want to enter a profession that requires a certification or degree. However, you will seldom get rich working at a job.

On the other hand, hiring a team member who has the school-learned skills to fast-track your business can be very beneficial to quick start and hyper-growth your business. An employee or partner with real skills behind the years of learning can help you eliminate unnecessary business mistakes.

Don't be afraid if you don't have what you think it takes academically because you can still launch your own business and learn as you grow or as said, you can hire someone who knows what you should be doing to help you facilitate your growth. The degree of your seriousness is what is most important!

Development

Get It Right From the Get Go!

As an entrepreneur, a big component of your initial work will be at the early development stage. Developing the necessary skills and plans will help to eliminate pitfalls and will also help you to fast-track your business.

The key to any successful business launch is developing strategic plans that include well-thought out marketing plans, a yearly budget, great team members, good location (if it's a brick and mortar business), and reliable suppliers. Your business development is also dependent on you, as the head of your company to be in the right frame of mind, in excellent physical condition, with strong family and social connections, as well as a spiritual foundation.

Part of your development is to check on licensing and tax matters, consult with experts (yes, even paid experts) and try to plan for any and all contingencies that may arise in the course of your early-stage enterprise. There are always numerous professional development conferences you can attend that are organized by trade groups in your industry. There you will learn the industry latest trends and make valuable contacts. All of these are key components in the developmental stage of your business launch.

Distinguish

Why You?

Make sure that your business has some very distinguishable traits, such as your logo, special brand awareness, unique packaging, original marketing, a recognizable uniform. You want to create a market advantage, whatever market you are entering. You want to be differentiated from your competition.

Sadly, a lot of what I see today lacks so much of this creative process. Sameness is so prevalent that it is hard to find similar products that have unique features that distinguish them from one another. How do you get your product or service above the general humdrum? If you can learn to apply your creative talent, however wild it may seem to your mom or dad, and distinguish yourself from all the other players in the game, you can truly accelerate your business growth.

Having a distinct look, feel and appeal will set you apart from others. Just think of some international brands such as FEDEX, Ferrari, Dom Perignon, Lady Gaga. How original or unique your product or service is today is very important with all the noise going on the internet, social media and the news. How does your product or service rise above all that noise? You can see that people gravitate toward products and ideas that are markedly different from all the rest of the products in their market. Be super creative in order to distinguish your business offering!

Dependable

This is Basic!

It is very important that people are able to depend on you for quality service and products, for your hours of operation, and for overall reliability. This may seem like an obvious principle for any successful business but sadly, some businesses shut down earlier than their schedules say or they don't open on time. They don't deliver products in a timely fashion, or correct whatever may be wrong.

All of these things are business killers that in time will destroy your operation. Therefore, as a knowledgeable and experienced entrepreneur, I say that you should never fall prey to these types of lapses if you want your business to survive and thrive.

Remember, that your competition is always behind you, next to you and in front of you. Being honest in your representation and dependable in your delivery is simply part of the basics if you want to give your business the opportunity to experience accelerated growth.

Divide

A Divided Attention?

Learn not just how to add up your receipts or subtract costs but also how to divide your gross revenues. I say this because you are definitely going to have to show a profit and loss statement that tells your accountant, the government and your investors where your revenue came from and where it went.

You are dividing all the money in your business to understand the whole money pie. On another level, you will have to divide employee hours for maximum return and minimal cost. And this kind of division has to be done in advance of any slower of more accelerated business times, such as before a holiday or after a holiday, whether you have seasonal or other types of fluctuations in your business, such as construction, employee illnesses, change of products or services.

As an entrepreneur, an owner and an employer, you had better learn to divide your attention in a concentrated and orderly manner in order to consider all the factors that may be gainfully or adversely affecting your business. This is commonly called multi-tasking think of yourself more like a general at the top of a hill watching the deployment of your troops in various formations in order to successfully defeat the enemy.

You have heard the expression, "Divide and conquer!" What is applicable in the military is oftentimes used strategically in business too. You are "wearing many hats" as the leader of your troops so be sure to divide your assets and resources in a manner that skillfully produces the goals of your strategic business plans.

Digest

To Assimilate or Not?

There will be times when there is information you haven't digested. For an entrepreneur, to digest means absorbing and understanding new information as it comes in real time. To digest that information means that you comprehend the present and oncoming significance of that data to your business.

Digesting information may require you to arrange something new in your system, discard something, increase here, reduce there, expand or contract in certain areas. To digest something physically, you must consume and break it down into parts that can be assimilated. This same principle applies to the business world.

You will find that it is very necessary at times to trim the fat in your business, allowing for growth by rejecting that which is not digestible. This also entails always looking for ways to curtail wasteful spending, avoiding wasteful by-products, e.g. in the manufacturing process, or sidestep generating unneeded expenses in your sales and marketing, e.g. ineffective advertising.

Learning to properly digest that which is beneficial to your business and remove that which cannot be digested is simply sound business practice for any thriving enterprise.

Diplomacy

How to Be Nice, *and* Effective!

I cannot stress enough the importance and meaning of diplomacy. From an entrepreneur's perspective, diplomacy means you have the capacity to deal with all sorts of people, customers and clients, employees and providers in sensitive and effective ways. Diplomacy is the art of dealing with people in a sensitive and effective way; speaking and acting with respect and empathy for another person. International statecraft is built on successful diplomacy.

Being an entrepreneur does not give you the license to say or do whatever you want because you own and run the company. I advise you not to take this approach. Instead, be willing to humble yourself and allow the customer to state any complaint about their experience with your product or service.

Customers or clients should not be made to feel as though they will be challenged or denied in their claims. Employees should not feel that they will criticized, ridiculed or fired for voicing their opinions. Part of the success of large, medium and small companies comes from taking the diplomatic approach, also known as "the customer is always right," whether they are or not. Diplomacy always means giving more, even to the point of "bending backwards" to please your customer, or "going the extra mile."

Diplomacy gives your clients the perception that you value them and that insures that they will continue to patronize your business. Nowadays, we have forgotten the old and true saying, "The customer is king!" Be diplomatic and be successful!

Defense

The Best Offense is a Good Defense!

Any sports coach can tell you that. You have to defend your basket, your goal post, or the ball. To defend means to protect something or someone. As an entrepreneur, what do you need to defend? It could be your employees or team members, your product or service, or your reputation. It could be your equipment.

All of these must be guarded because they are valuable. Insurance is one form of defense, security guards and cameras are another. Make sure that classified information stored on your computer is adequately protected. Be aware of what in your system can break down so you can be up-to-date on ways to protect all of your equipment.

Even though you are busy thinking about and working on moving your business forward at an accelerated growth, every once in a while peek in the rear view mirror or over to your side. It always helps to be a defensive driver.

E

Example

Be an Example!

As an entrepreneur, the example you display is of paramount importance for your business and potential customers and clients. There are segments of our population that will only do business with those who espouse their own values. People can see what you value based on the example you set before the world.

Demonstrating examples of love, leadership, honesty, and dependability will often guide people to your business. If you are seeking to launch or grow your business, I highly recommend that you start to identify your client base early on and then by example, start to match their needs and expectations at the basic levels. Trust me when I say that people are watching, talking, and waiting to see where you are coming from and that will either motivate them to follow you or to distance themselves from your product or service.

Being an exemplary figurehead of your organization itself definitely helps to propel your business forward. You should also train your team members by your example so that they too become exemplary models of the values that your company embodies. Always lead by example!

Examine

Keep Examining!

As an entrepreneur, you must never forget to continuously examine and re-examine your mission, goals, and vision for your business. Times change, and people change. Everything changes; therefore, if you are seeking to be at the forefront of what is happening in your particular industry, do regular examinations of your mission, goals and vision compared to current industry trends. This is vital for the survival of your business. Business is like a child in the sense that you are birthing something. Just as there have to be routine examinations for children growing up, so it is with your business. Things are moving at such an accelerated pace today that if you truly want to thrive you must stay on top of your business products and services. Give or request feedback from your customers as often as you can, for this is a major form of examination. Examine and re-examine yourself and your performance. Examine and re-examine your team's performance, your product or service's place in the market, your supply chains or service providers. You seriously cannot lapse into any complacent sense, even if all looks like it is moving along superbly. Keep vigilant at all times. Just like a captain of ship knows from his charts where there are shallow waters, rock outcroppings or other dangers, similarly you are in the wheelhouse of your entrepreneurial venture and you must continue to examine and

Explain

Explain Things!

Oftentimes your team members have an idea of what you want from them but it may not be an accurate understanding. Your business will be greatly enhanced and staff members will be able to deliver exactly what you want or need when you yourself have clarity within yourself. Do you really know what you want? Then you need to be able explain that in a cogent and articulate way so that each member of your team understands it, and can then carry out your orders plus project that idea accurately to your customers.

Learn to explain things in a timely fashion, and in a way that is clear, precise, and doable. That skill leads to positive progress in any business that functions in a systematic and orderly fashion. Explanations that are clear and concise allows your business to grow in a streamlined manner that also enhances the experience of your clients and customers. You have to be to explain well both verbally and in written form. The result is an improved bottom line.

Understand the importance of explaining your business in the classic "elevator pitch." That is the 10 second explanation about your business that you can present to anyone at any time, even if you are awakened by a phone call in the middle of the night by a prospective new client.

If you can explain your business goals in a mindful and distinct manner, whole new opportunities will open for your business.

Elect

Who Are You Electing?

As an entrepreneur, remember that when your business starts to thrive, there will be people in your organization vying for better positions, more territory and better compensation. Of course, that's a good sign but let me warn you that you must then become very mindful of the persons who you elect to be the faces of leadership in the public view and also who you elect to be the brains behind the scenes of your business.

Learn the importance of electing the right person for the right job is vital. Too often we entrepreneurs elect someone because he or she is a family member, has been on the team from inception or who may even be of a particular race or culture. While these factors may have some relevance, you must go beyond them to elect the perfect person for the position that needs to be filled.

I have experienced first-hand how I have elected someone who could not qualify for a position that I needed to fill and unfortunately found out that person could not handle their responsibilities. Obviously, this creates hard feelings when poor performance outcomes are the result of poor election skills.

In your election process, consider what skills a person really possesses, and their ability to understand and implement your business goals, vision, and mission. Simply put: Elect the right person for the job!

Effective

How to Be Effective!

Entrepreneurs, you want your partners, employees, customers and community to be able to see, feel and know how effective you are as a leader at following up and following through on your business model. Being effective means being operationally efficient and useful. Being effective within your industry sector means letting people see firsthand that what you say and do is aligned with your mission, vision, and goals.

Being effective and having the power to affect positive changes in your immediate jurisdiction, as well as the global community, creates trust and loyalty, plus good will and good word-of-mouth.

Be an effective communicator by knowing every detail of your product or service and being able to articulate every positive aspect of your business to anyone. Your business helps to make people's lives more effective, doesn't it?

I know that the effective way of doing business is relevant in today's marketplace, and so does my competition. Being foundationally effective means to never give up on knowing how you can bring about changes in the world for the betterment of humanity, personally and through your business.

Remember always the definition of effective: successful in producing a desired or intended result. Stick with your original mission, communicate well, stay mindful and healthy, be objective and always curious, and you will learn how to be a truly effective entrepreneur.

Enjoy

Enjoy and the World Enjoys With You!

I know firsthand how awful life can be some days in the business world, especially if you are not feeling fulfillment. Although money is a very relevant asset, I would suggest that you not go into any business merely for the money. If you can find what brings you and your client base the most joy, then I can guarantee to you with a degree of certainty that you will never feel like you are at work.

Most of us that are having fun and enjoying what we do seem to always be at play. Enjoy what you do. Knowing the value of what you do and how this affects others in a positive way will always vibrate joyfully within you and with others who meet you.

The ripple effect of a joyful and happy vibration go with you wherever you go, and align with whatever product or service you are selling. Others definitely feel that joy and they will want to be a part of what you are offering to the world. Try it!

Put some joy in your eyes and in your smile, and some bounce in your walk and sparkle in your talk and watch how people get interested in what you are selling them. Enjoy every moment!

Exit

Plan Your Exit!

Just like on airplanes, when they explain where the exit doors are, know your exit plan. Whether it be to pass the business on to your heirs or to sell the business, it is critical for you to have an exit strategy.

True entrepreneurs always have new ideas and they keep buying and selling new businesses. Unless you are forced to exit your venture, you want to gauge when your business is at maximum or peak profitability, Maybe that is the time for an exit in the form of a sale or an M&A (Merger & Acquisition) offer from a larger company. If you have the possibility of selling your business at a profit, or are cutting your losses, or simply passing the business on to family, you will make the proper preparations such as mentoring the next leader or new partner of the business.

In any case, it's always good practice to groom the leaders of your business should you suffer a personal demise. Know the dollar value of your business based on your years in creating the business, your client base, good will and other assets—all part of being prepared for an exit strategy. You never know; some competitor or M&A person may make a casual inquiry at a cocktail party and you should be already prepared to maximize your return through a well-thought out, substantiated and well-articulated exit plan.

Embellish

Make It Shine!

Embellish your brand! To embellish means to make it more attractive with some extra frills. Every detail of your business should be sparkling, in every aspect. From the moment you speak about the business or when people look up your website, or when they see an advertisement about your product or service, make sure they are fascinated by the whole presentation and every detail.

All of your images should be in sync with each other: brand, logo, graphic design. Your marketing materials are rich with content as part of the branding strategy. Your extra effort in the form of an embellishment helps the public note anything with your logo on it as special.

By example: Coca-Cola could have just used a plain font as their emblematic logo but that certain fancy little swirl in their font has been recognized internationally since 1886! Feel free to be fanciful and embellish!

Embark

It's a Journey!

Once you embark on this journey called entrepreneurship, you must prepare yourself for the long haul. There are American and global companies that have been around for centuries in every business sector.

I can tell you from some bitter business experiences, every business is going to face some ups and yes, some downs; some highs and some lows. That's the nature of business and of life, so you must have a 100 year business plan before you embark on the entrepreneurial journey. I'm serious!

A long term business plan will allow you to determine how you will start, continue and yes, even end your personal connection to the business, even though the business marches on through time.

Once you embark on your entrepreneurial adventure, look toward the infinite future of that adventure. Think to yourself and vision, what will this business look like in the future when my grandchildren are running it? Think about it: when anyone smart and ambitious embarks on a long term venture—think of Christopher Columbus, for example—what do they see beyond the horizon? Embark on your entrepreneurial venture with insight no end in sight!

Endure

How to Endure!

To endure means to know what we can tolerate through our experience. Often, we jump into the water, not realizing that there are both shallow and deep ends and that we must determine what part of the pool helps us to best endure in our environment. Be mindful that the deeper the water, the more sharks there are swimming around ready to devour the small fish. That's why it is so important to know where to jump in the pool.

If you try to swim with the sharks and you have not endured enough to become keenly aware of the nature of your surroundings, you will be eaten alive. Sharks typically prey and devour smaller, weaker fish.

Therefore, pace yourself, flow into growth and learn how to endure the ebb and flows that are customary in any industry. Research, consultations and developing your own intuition will guide you where to go and where not to go. Endurance is a measure of energy usage. In order to endure in your business, learn to measure your energy in the environment in which you are expending that energy.

For the longest and most effective endurance, always maintain your physical well-being, mental alertness and clarity, emotional stability, good social connections and your spiritual foundation. If you really follow this advice, you will do a lot more than endure—you will prosper and prevail!

F

Free! Free!

Giving It Away Has Huge Benefits!

As an entrepreneur, it is really truly okay to think freely and to give your all from a space of freedom. Often, entrepreneurs who are not truly and spiritually informed try to stay away from the word "free."

However, if you can find a way to formulate a product or service for your customer and you are able to give something away for free, you are highly likely to become a success. If you listen to most infomercials or advertisements you will hear of several different methods for sellers to add or give away something for free if the buyer is willing to do something to get the gift. This is a principle that works because it is based on giving.

Notice also that the biggest companies in the world are giving a lot away to their customers for free and that's called 'open source.' You don't pay for Facebook, Twitter, Wikipedia or Instagram, right? You don't pay for your Gmail, or your Google search, or YouTube. The entrepreneurs who built these business empires have understood right from the beginning the financial benefits of giving it away for free. And in turn they have become immensely wealthy owners and their companies have become the biggest and most profitable companies on earth.

Spiritual law states that as you give you shall receive. So, if you are seeking to accelerate and grow your business, please do not forget to give something for free and also to have a positive attitude about giving freely. Consider also that when you give a percentage of your total revenue to a charity (also called a tithe) you are both building community and feeling good about yourself too. Be free to give!

Fortune

Attract Good Fortune!

Entrepreneurs must want to create good fortune in your life and in the lives of others. When you understand this basic principle, you are definitely on the journey to success beyond measure. What you are telling the invisible power, who I call God, is: "I care for me and for others. I care that I operate with integrity. I care how people perceive me. I care that my product and service are helping to make the world a better place. I care that through my endeavors I get to enrich the lives of more people than myself."

Realize your good fortune in that you received an incredibly exciting entrepreneurial concept from somewhere. And realize your good fortune in finding the financing and the right personnel for this new and important product or service. Good fortune means the arrival of something or someone in a sudden or unexpected manner.

Some folks call it good luck but luck is more about superstition which has no place in business. I like to call these amazing moments a "fortunate situation" and I have come to realize these moments don't come by accident. You start working with the good intentions for the good fortune of all and I tell you that by the power of your good intentions, you will succeed.

Louis Pasteur said, "Fortune favors the prepared mind." This is about the Law of Attraction: As you want to create good fortune for others, the Universe will attract good fortune for you. The principle never changes and is always working for the universal good fortune. Opposing this universal principle is not advised! Stay with your original pure intentions and good fortune will find you.

Find

Find What You Need!

Entrepreneurs, learn the art and skill of finding what you need. When you seek, you will always find. Therefore, be astute in finding the partner for your business, the right brick and mortar location for your business or the right personnel for the services you provide. Find the right manufacturer for your product and find the right employees, the right accountant, the right lawyer, find the right permits, the right licenses.

There is an old expression, "The only ship that won't sail is a partnership." I strongly disagree with that because for those who originated their business with the wrong partner, some fault has to be blamed at their feet and not some bogus excuse. Find people with whom you can work together in alignment and synchronicity. And no, it is not "hard to find good help these days."

Maybe your intentions and your efforts have not initially found the right frequencies. Note that countless businesses find very good, dedicated associates and team members, professionals who are willing to do what's necessary to help the business to thrive. If you are not finding what you need, in a few moments of contemplative silence, ask yourself why that is. What quality within needs to be activated in order to find what you need? What quality within you needs to be abandoned? What quality that you already possess needs to be further activated?

Once you get on a visioning track such as this, you will be surprised to find the right answers come up from your inner wisdom voice. Soon enough you will find the right people and the right resources at the right time.

Funds

Finding Funds!

Entrepreneurs, where do you find the funds to launch your enterprise? Ha, that's a question that's as old as civilization. How you are going to fund your venture and also take care of yourself and your dependents?

If you are not using your own savings or credit cards to launch your business, you have to use OPM (Other People's Money). For initial funding, start by putting together a coherent and realistic business plan that itemizes all your need to effectively and successfully run your business for the first five years. Then, approach your banker, a private loan company, a venture capitalist group, an investment angel, your wealthy aunt or look into crowd-sourcing.

Writing business plans cannot be covered here but there are plenty of templates you can find on the internet. Seek counsel from someone you know who has raised funds for their enterprise. Check into crowd-funding. You must be creative!

Along the way, don't forget about the first law of nature: self-preservation. Set up your funding to include your own healthy salary and other forms of compensation. On the personal side, I have enough in my business plan not just to pay my rent and personal needs but my compensation allows me a retirement fund that includes my children's college fund, plus any golden parachute contingencies.

You must seriously study and understand the basic principles of funding if you want to lock in the steady growth and development of your business. If you take on a business partner, clearly define what their funding investment requires of them as well as what your duties will entail.

And remember as you are working on funding, don't forget to ask the Creator, the greatest funder of all enterprises, to help you in your quest to further your enterprise which is built on universal principles of engaging in the highest good. In these ways, you will be funded!

Fidelity

Learn and Practice Fidelity!

Fidelity is defined as faithfulness to a person, cause, or belief, demonstrated by continuing loyalty and support. There are so many unscrupulous dealings in the business world that you will encounter during your entrepreneurial career. It's not that people are good or bad but that some people have adopted the idea that they must get to the next level by any means necessary.

This is why athletes will use illegal substances to gain strength and power. Others will tell lies, and still others will steal. This is happening on every level of business, in government and all the way down to the person who is receiving a fraudulent welfare or a social security check. I have seen it all.

However, if you learn the principle of fidelity; that is, to faithfully and continuously operate from your moral intentions and to maintain your stated duties and obligations, your work and your ethics will not go unnoticed. Again, the Law of Attraction states that what you sow, that shall you reap. Sometimes you will not reap when or how you think you should, but you will certainly reap something worthwhile if you maintain fidelity to the highest good.

Feelings

Tune Into Your Feelings!

Entrepreneurs, be in touch with your deepest feelings! I like to call it, God speaking to you. I do not believe that your feelings ever lie to you. I'm not talking about common feelings. I am referring here to your gut feelings.

Are you aware that neuroscience has shown that we have the same type of neurons surrounding our gastrointestinal track as we have in our brains? When you are truly in touch with your feelings, you begin to know and perceive things before they even occur. You will know if someone means you harm or if they are not working in the best interest of the business. We're not talking about common feelings here like affection, anger, embarrassment, etc.

I can't emphasize enough how much further your business can grow when you are in touch with that invisible sensation within you called your gut feeling. I like to slow down in a place where I can be contemplative and allow my mind to quiet down. Then I ask my quiet mind what I should do, or where and when I should do this and that. That quiet place always has an answer for me through my feelings. I have been in situations where I felt my way through them just like a blind musician.

Pay attention to those gut reactions. Then assess things closer once you have tuned into that special place. Any successful entrepreneur will tell you stories of what happened when they did not listen to their gut feelings, and of the times when they did pay close attention to those feelings. Feelings must be seen as a vital part of the growth and success factor of your business.

Fertile

Understand Fertility

Entrepreneurs need to have an understanding of how to create fertile business conditions should produce an abundance of your product or service, the same as a fertile soil produces an abundance of healthy crops.

Be mindful that fertile grounds are where the harvesting takes place. This means you are doing everything in your power to plant and create the proper conditions for a fertile harvest. The various proper conditions for your business seeds and the timing of their seeding, your nurturing and careful growing of your product or service, harvesting and selling, all has to be carefully analyzed. The successful implementation of these processes will determine the maximum results that have been carefully executed by you and your team.

Create your checklist for the fertile conditions needed: Prepare a proper business plan, secure long term funding, gather together a great team, thoroughly research the market, know your suppliers, and implement smart sales and marketing strategies.

Check to make sure all of your i's are properly dotted and your t's are properly crossed to ensure that all your reasoning for that particular season is aligned for a bountiful harvest. Use this agricultural analogy for your business to succeed. Refer to the famous Parable of the Sower found in 3 of the New Testament gospels for even deeper inspiration on the importance of fertile grounds.

Familiarize

Know What is Happening!

Any successful entrepreneur must first familiarize themselves with their industry sector. Familiarize yourself with the latest trends, developments and leaders in your business. Familiarize yourself with the next wave of technology that could disrupt your industry positively or negatively, such as artificial intelligence (AI). What can be automated in your business, saving time for your human resources, streamlining product manufacturing or services?

Read your trade journals, know global macro-economic trends and how your business fits into larger patterns, attend and exhibit at trade conferences that keep you up-to-date with your competitors, and help you to make new contact plus meet new customers. It is a must that you always continue to familiarize yourself with everything that supports and furthers your business currently and in the future.

Favor

The Financial Value of Favors!

Entrepreneurs understand the importance in courting favors in business. This simply means you want to establish and maintain goodwill with your suppliers and clients. Remember, a favor is an act of kindness beyond what is due or usual.

I have enjoyed favors in most of my business endeavors simply because I have courted them. How have I courted favors? For one, I maintain a pleasant attitude toward everyone. I also go the extra mile for a supplier or client whenever I can do it. Something as simple as paying off a consignment deal or a loan before the expected time frame creates a little extra pleasantness in our business dealings.

You will discover that a little extra pleasantness oftentimes has a financial value down the road. Courting favor also includes a personal touch. For example, just a short inquiry as to how the supplier's or client's family is doing creates a certain friendliness beyond straight ahead business exchanges. Send greeting cards and salutations on holidays. This will bring benefits!

Recently, when there was an overstock of items that our business could use, the supplier contacted us first with a discounted offer for those items. We are on friendly terms and the supplier thought of us first when the opportunity came along. Small personal (or large) favors and gestures of thoughtfulness by you and your personnel who are also trained by you to understand the importance of favors will be translated into profits. You can never lose with this favorite principle of mine!

G

Glorify

Put a Real Shine on It!

As an entrepreneur, always glorify your business, product, and services! Describe or represent every part of your business as admirable and praiseworthy. You should speak good and only good about every aspect of your business as much as possible, to anyone possible. This is free advertising and a true marketing component that should not be left out of the equation.

Glorify the good work of your team members and managers; glorify the sales force, glorify and uplift every person on your team from the maintenance crew to the VP's, those who are bigger or smaller components of your entrepreneurial empire, because they are all imperative to the ultimate success of your business.

Remember that the small screw is what holds the great beam in place. So, as you move forward, always remember to glorify, generously compensate, and activate the potentials and the results of each team member. Your investors, client and customer, suppliers, all need to be glorified. If there is a letdown, as the fearless leader of your troops, continue to hold and articulate the bigger picture, and at the same time continue to inspire anyone who has not performed to their full potential to see the glory in that bigger picture and their part in it.

To glorify means to visibly polish and make sparkle all the good that your company represents to itself and publicly. Glory comes to those who seek the ultimate best!

Genuine

Be Real!

For some time I lived in Hollywood, Tinsel Town, as they call that part of Los Angeles, California. This is the land of movie making, women chasing, expensive cars and multinational entertainment companies. Trust me when I tell you about the many people in this place who are not genuine and act out so many different roles that they change their masks in what seem like moment by moment flashes. I met very few people that I could say were truly genuine. Instead, most people were hiding their true identity.

I know all about this ingenuous way of being because I was one of those persons, not wanting people to see me for who I really was because I feared and wondered what people would, say, or think if I was my authentic self.

I found out in a painful way that we do ourselves a disservice when we can't be genuine or authentic. Listen up, fellow entrepreneurs! The sooner we can be open, honest and real, the faster we can become free from the mental and physical strains that we place on ourselves which keep us from being a true success.

Being genuine is our true nature but oftentimes feelings of lack, insecurity, embarrassment and retribution cause us to be phony, to make misrepresentations, not to follow through, to lose valuable trust and ultimately kill our business and our reputation.

Remember the old wisdom saying, "Know thyself, and to thine own self be true!" This is should your genuine starting and end point in business and in life.

Guarantee

Prove You Believe in Your Business!

Your brand or company is well served if you can guarantee your product or service, and then truly back it up. I've come to realize that if you are in business and seeking to remain for the long haul, you need to find out what parts of your product or service you can guarantee to your customers.

People love to do business with folks and companies that can stand up to their word and deliver on their promises. If you have ever heard the Men's Wearhouse advertisement, you will remember that the last words the CEO/spokesperson George Zimmer says, "You're gonna like the way you look. I guarantee it." That brand became nationally recognized, resulting in many, many people shopping there, I believe, mainly because of George's personal and authentic guarantee. Think about it, when the CEO of a company appears in front of the camera, looks directly at you and guarantees his product, how many people will doubt his word?

Make a guarantee on your product or services to your customer. That guarantee instills confidence in your product, service and company. Give a quality guarantee or a price guarantee. Find something with your product or service to guarantee. It only makes sense that a company who advertises their guarantees will sell more product or service, and will attract more new customers than a company who doesn't guarantee what it sells. Does that make sense, entrepreneurs?

Goal

Scoring Goals!

Every entrepreneur understands the importance and power of setting goals. Goals are a way of measuring, examining, and achieving the vision you have implemented for the growth and success of your business. You should set goals for product launches, including dates, sales and service strategies, outcome expectations, reinvestments.

Remember that your business growth is highly dependent upon the goals you set and how you go about to achieve your goals. Write down and review all the objectives that you want to accomplish with the business. Make the vision plain so you can explain it to your grandma. Set down the stages for the achievement of your goals. Prioritize goals through analyzing the order and timeliness in which your goals need to be completed.

Be realistic, as well as somewhat quixotic, in order to make your goals manageable at early stages in your business as well as when your business matures. Once you reach your goals, it's always a good time to break out the champagne! Then, get back as soon as possible, to setting new and even bigger goals.

Growth

Out of the Gate!

All of life is about growth, unfolding, and well-being. Look at the rose seed. It grows into a bush and out of the branches grow beautiful roses. Nature in the plant, animal, human and cosmic reality is about never-ending evolution and growth.

Entrepreneurs, if you are planning to launch a product or service, plan well how you want your manifest vision to grow. If it is not growing, it's dying. Anything that has growth potential should become invigorated with the right conditions for maximum growth. Everything in life has a growth span but some species and some businesses have learned the art of sticking around for a long, long time.

Can you grow a business forever? Maybe not, but we can look to growing our business for our life span and for our heirs. The growth of your business begins with assessments and actions that show you an upward swing on the graph of your business. Growth in the early stages of your business has to be carefully monitored and evaluated. Keeping your attention firmly on the first stage of the rocket booster tells you the trajectory of your business path.

Entrepreneurial efforts that succeed depend on steady and reliable growth, as chaperoned closely by you the owner and your team. If any unwelcome deviation from your early stage goals becomes apparent, change direction in a timely manner and continuing growing a new and better way.

Guide

Allow for Guidance!

As an entrepreneur, you are the one who is responsible to guide your business and watch where it is going. Oftentimes, we entrepreneurs get stuck along the journey at various points. Be open to guidance. At some juncture along the way, you may stray off course and you will need to be pointed in the right direction again. Even airline pilots have computer and human guides. Air traffic controllers monitor and help correct course for the pilots.

Business guides come in many forms, so be open and receptive. Your guide may be a paid consultant, your corporate board, an author of a business book, your successful business aunt, or some esoteric message in a dream. Just ask for guidance when you need it and you'll be amazed at who shows up to help you.

Don't get too egotistical in your position of power that you do not develop the necessary trait to be able ask for help when you need it. When you don't need specific help, ask for feedback. Feedback from customers and employees serves the very important function of evaluating your business, and consequently guiding your course. You need to always be guiding your business and allow for guidance to know how far you've come along your entrepreneurial journey, and where a course shift may be required.

Governing

Know the Governances!

In the United States and in every country that you will be doing business, there are various governing bodies that determine what businesses can and cannot do. City, state, and federal regulations govern business requirements, such as licensing and permits, taxes and how to comply with legally set standards for your industry. This means that you have to do the necessary due diligence, do the research, learn the rules, regulations, laws, and guidelines before you leap into your entrepreneurial adventure.

Not knowing the governing laws and the bodies that enforce the laws in your state or city is not an excuse before these governing agencies not to impose back taxes, penalties and fines on you, and possibly denying you from doing business under their jurisdiction. Reach out to these agencies and don't rely on hearsay, or trying to avoid the regulations.

Be informed from the get-go on what the governance rules are so that you can keep governance over your business affairs without any unneeded disruptions to your thriving enterprise.

Generosity

Generosity Pays!

Entrepreneurs need to learn right from the start that generosity is a simple habit that can be developed to fortify your business. When you are generous to your clients and customers, they take notice and want to do business with you.

A friendly smile with a "Hello, and how are you today?" or "How is your family?" are all simple words that are demonstrate a generous nature and have powerful results. Don't forget to use these simple words which will bring an increase of sales to your business and sales. Sending an email or text message or making a call to say hello really does go a long way, as does getting together for a round of golf or inviting a prospective client for a drink—and paying for it!

Give your product or services generously to charities whenever you have the opportunity to do so. Those kinds of gestures make new customers for you and word-of- mouth spreads about the great quality of your product. Gifts at Christmas are seen as a generous gesture by your clients. These are cost-effective marketing and advertising tools. So, learn to be generous and you will attract the endless generosity of the Universe to you and your business. Give and ye shall receive!

Greatness

Plug Into Your Greatness!

I feel fortunate when I meet a business person who strives for greatness. Every entrepreneur, and even every non-business person, that I have encountered who strove for greatness has achieved success beyond their expectations. Greatness is that power that lies waiting to be discovered and manifested within each human being regardless of gender, color, ethnicity, nationality, age or sexual preference.

I am often reminded of motivational teacher Les Brown's saying that you have something special about you, and that there is greatness within you. The thing about the greatness within is that it must be unloaded and activated.

It's just like electricity—only useful when it is plugged in. Greatness, like electricity, is always available but we have to learn to connect with it, harness it and direct it. Then, we can take advantage of the tremendous things that electricity allows us to do.

Likewise, as we work to harness our inner greatness, many great things will be accomplished. How to get in touch with your individual greatness? Every day, do your morning meditation, your affirmations and your visioning. Eat well and maintain your physical excellence. Read worthwhile books, have a spiritual community and healthy social relationships, and learn to lead your team by wholesome example. Great things are definitely in store for those who have the courage to tap into their innate greatness.

Gifted

Use Your Gifts!

As an entrepreneur, you have been gifted with a very special aptitude: the willingness to take a risk. Lots of people will not risk much at all, preferring to stay in their comfort zone which is often encumbered by a limited belief system. But I say, "Go for it!"

You must use your God-given gifts because we are on this physical plane to be a blessing to others. And we all can be a blessing once we decide to release our gifts and talent onto the world stage and go for our destiny. So much unused talent goes to waste every single day.

Potential doctors, attorneys, artists, teachers and others miss their calling. And of course, anyone who has not been able to express their gifts and develop their full potential will have a list of very reasonable external circumstances to blame for their stunted growth. My own pastor defines blasphemy as not using the God-given gifts you were born with, and thus truly insulting God.

Discover and use your gifts in order to be fruitful in your entrepreneurial endeavors, and to share your gift with the world. Not only will you be blessed, you will feel good about yourself and be well-positioned to become well-compensated in your business, personal, social and spiritual life.

H

Habits

Develop the Right Ones!

Entrepreneurs must know that we are all provided for by God. However, because of what we see and hear, we tend to pick up certain human habits, whether good or bad. A habit is something that we become accustomed to doing on a regular basis. Habits of survival are hardwired into us but we must also develop habits that go beyond these basic instincts.

I know that it is challenging for us to act according to all the natural good that God has provided for all of us because of our various early conditionings. Certain habits that do not serve our good nor the collective good are created over the years. Therefore, be mindful of what you are constantly thinking, saying and doing because thoughts and words become habits that become your destiny.

Once something is locked in the subconscious mind, it influences your actions. If habits develop that do not serve you, your community, your employees, your clients or your entrepreneurial goals, all is for naught. Unconscious habits can lead to disaster.

Learn from the get-go to create and maintain the right kinds of habits: Seeing realistic perspectives, not ones based on some prejudiced views; keeping to your goals while allowing for needed adjustments, and always pausing for self-reflection and guidance from the signs and miracles that are abounding all around you. Developing right habits will help you to become an effective entrepreneur.

Happiness

Creating and Maintaining Happiness!

Happiness is a way of being and as an entrepreneur, I find it helpful to maintain a constant state of happiness. When you can wake up happy and extend that happiness vibration all throughout the day, you will see how quickly others will gravitate to you and be willing to assist you in your entrepreneurial endeavors.

A happy feeling is contagious, and this is a point that I cannot stress enough. We all need more of this vibration. Whether sales are up or down, if you will maintain at the very minimum a constant state of inner happiness, everything you need will flow into that vibration. How do I maintain my inner state of happiness?

Every morning, whatever my personal, social or business situation, I recite out loud my day's intentions which include universal goals, personal and community goals, and my day's business goals. Having full trust in God knowing my pure intentions, I feel happy and energized. This simple exercise every single morning, weekends included, will certainly allow your business to grow and prosper, and help you to maintain that real God-given happiness. Try it!

Health

Health is Wealth!

Be mindful that not just your finances and those of others are at stake as an entrepreneur. Your health is also at stake because there will be all kinds of stress hitting your body and mind, particularly at the beginning of your enterprise. It is most important that you maintain your health because your health is your wealth.

The fundamental order for a healthy dispensation is proper exercise, diet, and mindfulness. Almost daily, you should include activities that induce cardio and aerobics, yoga, running, swimming, lifting weights, dancing, Zumba, tai chi and other fun physical activities that will help you live a healthy lifestyle. Watch your diet! Beware of drinking alcohol after 'a hard day at the office' or eating too much comfort foods like fried carbs or processed meats.

Eat your vegetables, as Mom says. I am a fan of veganism and vegetarianism because plant-based dieting is a healthier alternative to the excessive protein, sugar and starches in our diets. Take your vitamins and mineral supplements!

Of course the subject of health must include emotional health, mental health, spiritual health, and having a healthy social life. Obviously, an overall health plan needs to be part of your personal and professional business life. As an entrepreneur, you will notice a cleaner and higher energy on all levels when you are mindful of your health and well-being.

This important factor of vigor and strength allows you to do more and to have a greater capacity to go the extra mile when necessary. Think of yourself as a business athlete and always maintain your health!

Humble

Find Your Humility!

I have to admit that being humble is a big challenge for me. We entrepreneurs consider ourselves to be The Boss, The Big Shot, The Chief that everybody should obey and admire. Ha, after a few initial successes, you may start to get somewhat inflated about yourself and your talents.

However, I can tell you from some unpleasant embarrassments and let-downs over the span of my business career, the faster you realize the importance of humility, the sooner a certain measure of assuredness will be activated within you and you will really be able to be seen and admired as a trusted and effective leader.

Start simply by being grateful for all that you have been blessed with in your business venture, particularly in regard to the human and capital resources that God has helped you to assemble. Be thankful for every positive, and yes even sometimes the negative events that occur in your enterprise.

A humble person learns every moment, from everyone and every event, even from something as insignificant as a rock. I am not saying that you have to become a pushover or a yes-man or woman. I am saying that humility is the art of being cool, calm, and collected when you are under pressure or when things appear to be out of control and the challenges are mounting.

Understanding the importance of being humble, as I have humbly learned, will surprise you in the powerful and beneficial outcomes you will personally reap and in how your enterprise will exponentially succeed.

Heed

Take Serious Heed!

Take heed! To take heed means to be keenly aware of any danger that may lurk around you. Heeding the call to step up and out onto the world stage as an entrepreneur is vitally important and should be of serious concern to you even before you start to launch and build your product or service empire.

Take heed of your investors. Take heed of your operations manager, the person who is charged with running the daily affairs of your company. Take heed of the various managers who oversee the various departments in your company. Take heed of your manufacturers or service providers, your sales and marketing teams, your delivery systems, even your maintenance personnel.

You are ultimately responsible for every aspect of your enterprise because you hired those people and charged them with fulfilling the responsibilities you outlined clearly to them at the onset of their term.

To heed literally means to regard something with great care and concern. Heeding all the pitfalls or dysfunctional aspects of your enterprise early on will fast track your product or service, and save you from making costly mistakes.

Hopeful

Understand Hope!

Being hopeful is mandatory, personally and in business. To be hopeful means to have the faith to implement and put your systems in proper order so your business will thrive and not merely survive. Be mindful that being hopeful means you expect to receive that which you desire in life and business.

Being hopeful is a principle that allows you to be open and receptive to all the good that is already present all around you. Being hopeful is faith in action. Faith is the belief that you know that something is already available. Of course, you must take the necessary actions to bring that something into reality.

Hope is not magical thinking. When you have hope, meaning faith and belief that you can accomplish anything and you start to move in the direction of your hoped-for goal, you can only succeed. In being hopeful you are bringing forth and attracting the invisible structural substance of the Universe that manifests all material realities.

Hope is one of the foundational and most powerful forces of your budding and maturing enterprise. Without hope, everything is lost. Never give up hope!

Harness

Harness It All Together!

You will need to harness all of the forces and principles necessary to create the proper system for your business to run in an orderly fashion. Every system starts with a principle which is defined as a fundamental truth that serves as the foundation for a structure of belief or behavior, or for a chain of reasoning.

As you understand and obtain a vision of the proper order of things through your business principles, you will see that in reality all things are truly possible. Once you harness that vision and your principles to the methodology you devise in order to accomplish your business goals, your business success will commence.

Harness yourself to that methodology, which are your basic principles adapted as the blueprint for and the means for your enterprise's triumphs through your human and venture capital plus your other various resources. Your product or service will take off beyond your wildest expectations, and you will have a model that you can harness for replication purposes as well.

Your ability to harness the various elements of your business assures the continuation and growth of your enterprise locally, nationally and globally.

Humanity

Become a Humanist!

As an entrepreneur, always know that you are in the business of bringing a product or service to the marketplace for the greater good of humanity. Our humanity connects us. We are all interdependent. Our entrepreneurial enterprise must be seen as a holistic good that we can render to others.

This must become a key principle, whether you open a plumbing business or a non-profit social service. Factor humanity into any entrepreneurial endeavor. Humanity must be integrated into your basic understanding of why you are doing what you do.

Making humanity's concerns part of my business goals, I have experienced how the forces of the Universe have aligned with me and my efforts. God needs our help! Remember that all of life is about humanity evolving to its fullest and highest potential. Humanity can and will be restored to its natural state of being; a state in which there is a just and peaceful order.

Become mindful of our oneness with the whole of life. Understanding our common bond is another fundamental principle that will engender success for yourself and your family, for the families of your employees and for the family of man, sustaining all of us in the most idealistic and ultimately realistic mutual happiness. Learn to be human!

Helpful

Be Helpful!

Yes, our entrepreneurial and personal mission in life is to be helpful to others, as well as ourselves. As I travel about this earth on my business and personal journey of transformation, I am mindful that all of us are here to help each other according to our gifts and talents. The more we realize this truth, the faster we can be in the business of truly helping others, and seeing success coming toward us.

This insight into the truth of helping others has been demonstrated to me time and time again. When I took the time to be helpful to others, I was always rewarded even though I was not looking for any compensation. The Universe has a dualistic nature, one that operates on a give and receive basis. "As you give, so shall you receive." Or, we can put it this way, "As you help, so shall you be helped."

And remember that there are many ways to help others through your enterprise. Give help to your family and friends, to your employees, clients and community wherever and however you are asked to do so. Don't be stingy in your help. Help in a generous and happy way. Never expect compensation for your help but be very grateful when you see the exponential returns that the Universe eventually provides for your business and for yourself personally.

I

Invest

What Are You Willing to Invest?

As an entrepreneur, of course you must be keenly aware of when to invest, where to invest, and why you should invest. These are some questions that you want to contemplate before you sink your money or other people's money into your enterprise. Your investors will certainly want to know your answers to these questions.

Know that as an entrepreneur it is imperative that you have real 'skin in the game,' as the saying goes. Demonstrating the depth of your personal investment in your business shows your investors the depths of your commitment. Your investor, who is your future partner, is going to look deep into your eyes to determine if they are making the right investment that can lead to a profitable business or product launch.

That determination is based on several external factors of course but the foundation of any investment is ultimately based on your personal investment in the enterprise. How much time and money are you investing? How much of your energy and long term commitment are you investing? You need to be able to clearly articulate the investment you are willing to make in order for you to be taken seriously as a bona fide entrepreneur.

Know the answers to the questions you will be asked concerning each area of it that needs an investment of cash, human capital and all the other resources needed for your investment to bring in that much anticipated ROI (Return on Investment)

Increments

A Step at a Time!

As an entrepreneur, know that change is inevitable. Be mindful of the importance of tackling change incrementally. Changes here and there are what allow you to progress skillfully toward the goal post.

This is somewhat like a football game: You gain a few yards as you advance down the field toward achieving a first down. Therefore, be mindful that you don't expect to charge down the field at full force in a straight line. Progress always comes incrementally, a nice spurt of sales here and a slack time there.

Taking incremental steps at the opportune time will help you to flow past the naysayers, the competition and market vagaries. Most entrepreneurs are excited about their enterprise and like to move as fast as possible. I like the slogan, "Slow and steady." Remember who the winner is in the famous fable about the race between the tortoise and the rabbit. That incremental pace allows you to get to where you're headed with your business. Step-by-step, right move by right move, is the progressive, incremental pace that you want to take.

Industry

Know Your Industry!

You must know your industry sector and realize the impact that it has on the world. Once you have a concept of what is going on in your industry, you can seek to bring about necessary changes to help transform life on a global scale for the better.

All of life is on a growth pattern, and you as the innovator and creator have the duty to bring about the new technology in your industry that has the greater good of humanity at the forefront. Every industry has the capacity for creating positive change, and everything will not only change but must change. This is another Universal law that must be factored into every consideration of the product or service you are purveying in your industry.

All things change from old to new, and sometimes even from new to old. Those who are first to the marketplace are not always the ones with the greatest opportunity to reap the financial rewards. Always be on the lookout for the necessary changes that are taking place in your industry. Attend industry conferences to get the latest info on new developments, products and services being offered, as well as for the useful contacts you will make at those conferences. Consider taking an exhibition booth at the conferences.

Sometimes you may 'not see the forest for the trees.' That signifies that sometimes pulling back and getting a better perspective on your industry will propel you forward in a way that your competitors have not evaluated on acted upon. Know your industry!

Illustrate

A Picture is Worth a Thousand Words!

Entrepreneurs must be aware of illustrating their concepts and expectations clearly for themselves, their investors, their team, their clients and the public at large. Clearly illustrating your vision is important for the cultivation of harmony and order in your own house which is the base for all of your success.

Sometimes this concept of simply illustrating your product or service may become muddled or over-complex. I am sure you have also watched commercials on TV and after they finish, you are scratching your head and wondering what the message is they were trying to convey about their offering.

It is difficult for any business to flourish if there is no illustration of what is required of your team members. To illustrate means to make something clear or to explain it in a way that the team can follow, whether by example, by charts and numbers, even by a competitor's product.

Your team needs to grasp the aspirations, goals, and vision of the business. Provide clear examples of what you are talking about by illustrating in simple and understandable ways what thorough quality control takes, what proper packaging looks like, how an employee answers the phone, what your dress code reflects about your company.

The more you can illustrate your entrepreneurial concepts for your team, the easier your leadership role becomes as the team then carries those clear ideas into their work and as they distinctly disseminate your vision to the public.

Illuminate

Light Your Light!

As an entrepreneur, from birth you have been endowed, gifted, and blessed with a light, a gift and a talent that illuminates what you came here to do on earth. Indeed, all of us are born with an individual innate light that wants to burst forth to fulfill our mission here. That light can be utilized in many ways and also used commercially. Know what you want and need to do for others with that inner illumination, especially in the form of creating products and launching services that will help others along their life's journey.

We must understand, evoke and perform our entrepreneurial tasks with that spirit. Your illumined mind must be filled with the thought of illuminating other folks' minds, bodies and spirit when they use the product or service you offer them. Even selling something as mundane as an auto glass squeegee is illuminating!

Once we can conceive of the notion of an illuminated world, where darkness is dispelled, the right success will come into being with the product or service that flows from this kind of consciousness. When illumined minds touch one another, a domino effect is created throughout humanity. One light, lights another, then another, and the world just keeps getting bigger, better, and brighter.

Therefore, we must begin our entrepreneurial careers with getting ourselves illuminated from within. Being that light that we want to see in the world, and then keeping a vision of the whole of humanity sparking up, illuminated and acting with love to revolutionize the world for the better. Find your inner illumination and let it shine!

Impact

What Impact Will You Have?

Ask yourself, "What do I want to impact?" Ask yourself, "Why it is necessary for me to impact anyone else?" Ask yourself, "How can I best impact others with my product or service?" Ask yourself, "How will my enterprise impact others on a global scale?"

As an entrepreneur, realize that our world is in need of products and services that can benefit mass segments of the population, and that can be affordable and sustainable. As our earth population grows, resources get reduced. The climate will continue to change for the worse before it gets better, however optimistic we may be. Our world is becoming more and more connected through the advent of technology, artificial intelligence (AI), and mass communication, and things are not about to slow down. Through the impact of the human genome project and all the wonderful scientific benefits we are accruing by the day, people all over the world are living longer and connecting on a larger and more massive scale.

So, here is my question to you, my entrepreneurial friend, "What can you create that will impact humanity on the highest and best levels?" As you contemplate your product or service, think about the impact that it will have on the largest scale. Taking your scaled-up global perspective seriously will yield impactful results beyond your wildest imagination!

J

Jeopardy

It's Not the Name of a Game!

By definition, an entrepreneur is a risk taker. However, a skillful risk taker is a person who calculates the risks ahead of time and who skillfully avoids jeopardy. Jeopardy is defined as a state of danger, loss, harm, or failure. To jeopardize means to create danger, loss, harm of failure.

Jeopardy can occur because of an entire plan or one part of a plan. You can lose everything that you have sacrificed by making one stupid mistake. I highly commend the entrepreneurs who weigh their options and move forward in the most calculated manner possible. A calculated risk is one in which you have done your due diligence by surveying the marketplace and taking into account what other people within your industry are doing and how well they are doing it.

You should survey and measure the playing field by means of constructive and critical analysis. This basic principle of preparation will prevent you from jeopardizing all that you are working for and it will also minimize any loss that you might incur along your way to success. A skillful, professional gambler goes into the casino to win, and there is nothing casual about his determination even if he looks calm and collected. By contrast, gambling addicts are ultimately only looking to self-sabotage and put themselves in jeopardy.

As an entrepreneur, you are playing to win, and the way to do that is to avoid jeopardy. The way to do that is to always be prepared for it. Tread warily in order to circumvent jeopardy!

Job

It's Not a Job!

As an entrepreneur, please understand that your business is more than a job. Entrepreneurs are the vital force that goad the American and global economy forward. For salaried people, too often the word job is only the acronym J.O.B standing for "just over broke."

From the entrepreneur's vantage point, however, we create opportunities as we work to bring about a greater good through our desires to create products and services that enhance the lives of people all over the globe. Once you consider the importance of your purpose, be relentless in your pursuit, and don't take the notion that what you are embarking on is just another job.

For an entrepreneur jobs are boring, usually a dead end, and realistically more and more jobs are being automated anyway. The entrepreneur seeks to create positive and exciting changes that impact the entire world. Your focus and primary goal when you wake up each day to engage in your enterprise should be: My product or service will make a real difference in people's lives.

You will never hear a true entrepreneur use the expression TGIF ("Thank God It's Friday"). An entrepreneur wants to and is prepared to work 100 hours per week, not just 40. In Silicon Valley, where many of the wealthiest entrepreneurs in America got their start, there is a saying: "100 hours a week shows sincerity. 150 hours a week shows commitment."

Of course, I am not recommending that you work yourself to death. Obviously, no ordinary worker at their job would put up with that kind of work ethic but again, entrepreneurs don't do jobs. However, one day when you are ready to depart this earthly realm, you may hear a distant voice say, "Job well done!"

Joy

Why Are You Really Doing All This?

As an entrepreneur myself, I can say that choosing the life of an entrepreneur is a true blessing, a life full of joy. Joy is something that is embedded in each person on the planet from birth. Joy is our birthright, our natural state of being. However, we must activate and harness this innate joy and bring it into manifestation for the highest good.

Joy is the emotion that excites or ignites the energy of happiness, goodness and true success. To be in a joyful state of mind on a regular basis brings a flow of real good to your clients and customers. Your joy will create an appreciation in your clients and they will feel that it is a pleasure for them to engage in business with you.

Learn to honestly exude your joy in what you are offering the public. Know what brings out the joy in your life. I suggest that you delve into an industry that is congruent with what personally brings you joy. If you love to groom pets, people will notice that quality in your tone of voice and in your work product. They will feel confident in handing over their precious pets to you for service.

Life is supposed to be enjoyed so feel the joy in what brings you income. A joyful attitude will sustain you when challenges arrive. If you have not experienced this required joy, then reflect on how to make this magical, energetic resource start to bubble within you. Soon you will notice how this joy principle attracts customers and clients to you, and how your business grows and flourishes. Feel the joy!

Juggle

Learn the Art of Juggling!

As entrepreneur you need to develop the skills of a juggler. There will be times when you are going to have to carry others' load. For example, you might have to be the sales and marketing representative, the accountant and maintenance personnel, the chief and bottle washer, as the expression goes. You may be juggling numerous jobs, especially at the start of your enterprise.

As your business grows, sometimes positions will be left open by employees who leave, and you will have to fill in the void until you hire a replacement. This means you need to know how to handle as many aspects of your business as possible. I have a friend who owns an art gallery and he can sell art, teach you art history, plus hang and light a painting perfectly.

In my own various enterprises, I have had to juggle the jobs of buyer, market strategist, sales rep and in some cases, the janitor and stock person. Be mindful that along your entrepreneurial journey, it is inevitable that you will be called upon to juggle several jobs at once.

Possessing as many skills as possible in your enterprise is an asset and having a mindset of a juggler will serve you well in terms of growing your business.

Journey

It is Going to Be a Journey!

For an entrepreneur, the journey is never over. You are traveling from one phase to the next. Along this journey, you will encounter good and not-so-good times as life and its events are always shifting and changing. Are you really in it for the long haul? Do you really have the energy and endurance?

As you travel along the entrepreneurial road, stay focused and mindful that what you are doing is in sync with your purpose. Remember that what you are doing is making a mighty difference on this planet. Restate your intentions, purpose and goals as often as possible along the journey. The entrepreneurial journey is truly worth the time and effort as you continue to pursue your dreams and passions.

Your livelihood is one of the most important factors of your life so strive to make your journey sweet and worthwhile. Where the journey leads is never really foreseeable as new and sometime unpredictable other options become available to you. Hey, that's always going to be part of the journey!

Know your vision, stick with it and watch how the journey unfolds beautifully for you, your partners and employees, your family and friends, and your community.

Join

Who is Joining You?

As an entrepreneur, you want to join with like-minded people who also want to be successful, and see you become successful. How do you do this? If you are religious, join with the folks in your own church or temple to share your entrepreneurial vision, as well as your product or service. Join international fraternal organizations who engage in the same charitable projects and activities that also interest you.

Most cities and towns have a chamber of commerce which I suggest that you join. I have joined several trade organizations, national and global, affiliating with others who are helpful in furthering my business goals. Such organizations will give you opportunities to talk with and question some of the leaders in your industry and this will speed up your exponential growth.

Do the internet searches for joining with like-minded business people, who may even become your social friends too. Doing it all alone is the more difficult way, so join up with others wherever you see the benefits.

Journal

The Importance of Journaling!

Keeping a journal will accomplish several positive things for yourself and your business. First, you will have a document to look at from time-to-time to see your progress. Second, journaling allows you to outline the direction that you want to take your business.

Third, a journal provides a blueprint that reveals your formula for success to your heirs or successors. Fourth, journaling is an introspective process where you make for a private space to capture all the important clues, conceptions and perceptions that are useful in moving forward with your enterprise.

Start today to get a personal journal in order to crystallize all the significant data coming from your external impressions as well as your own inner creativity. You'll be surprised at how the very simple tool of a journal can help manifest and grow your business goals.

Jargon

Talk the Talk!

As an entrepreneur, you must understand the jargon used by your industry. Jargon constitutes the specific terms that a certain industry uses to quickly communicate when they are together. Doctors, lawyers, insurance agents, stock brokers, real estate brokers, restaurateurs, athletes and a host of other industry specialists—all use a particular verbal shorthand that lets them know they are dealing with professional colleagues.

Learn and understand the language of your industry because this knowledge will help others in the industry treat you favorably as an associate, not as an outsider. I have found that at times when I was not familiar with a particular industry's jargon, I might be overcharged. Be in the know!

Having been in the jewelry sales business for a number of years, I became familiar with the particular jargon that jewelers use when buying and selling precious stones or minerals, and this was tremendously helpful to me in doing business in that lucrative world. You recall the saying, "It's always good to know a second language." Know your jargon!

K

Knucklehead

Knuckleheads Cannot Succeed!

As an entrepreneur, be advised and be cautioned not to be a knucklehead. A knucklehead is a foolish or stupid person. A stupid person is one who hurts himself or herself, thereby hurting others. A knucklehead is a joke. It is very hard to be a successful, prosperous entrepreneur while at the same time being a knucklehead.

I know this because at one time I was a knucklehead myself. You know the old saying, "Everybody plays the fool; no exceptions to the rule." The key, though, is to not continue on the path of foolishness because it only sets you up for failure. Out of ignorance, we may play the role of a fool sometimes but to be stupid is to continue to do that which doesn't serve you nor benefit humanity.

As you work hard to become a successful entrepreneur, to become a better person and to serve the greater good, I implore you to listen to the indwelling Presence that is always active within each of us to guide us in the right direction for the highest good. At some point each of us has to grow up and give up our sophomoric behaviors and immature, selfish ways.

The law of attraction is always honest and true. If you are creating turbulence as a knucklehead, expect that the Universe will play a greater knucklehead to you and your entrepreneurial endeavors. In a word, don't be a knucklehead!

Knowing

Know How to Know!

As an entrepreneur who has launched and been involved with the development of several products, I can attest that knowing how to know is very important. The first knowing and absolute best knowing is having that inner knowing which flows from your intuition, also known as insight.

The second knowing is being informed that something is about to take shape, also known as foresight. This is maybe the most powerful form of knowing. For example, your city council members determine the laws and set the practices for entrepreneurs that do business in their city. Knowing this valuable information ahead of your competitors should motivate you to consider knowing what the coming trends are that will affect your business. Maybe you need to be in step with those who know, even by hobnobbing with them and attending the policy-setting council meetings that shape your industry.

The third knowing occurs when you learn something through hindsight. For example, you may recognize a particular trend that in hindsight you should have known about to help you get ahead of your competition. Once you know something, own it so that you can start to make better choices and decisions about your enterprise.

Knack

Have or Develop a Knack!

I like the word "knack" simply because of its profound meaning: to have a clever way of doing something. The word reminds me of a bible scripture that states we should be wise as a serpent but harmless as a dove. To have a knack means that you employ wise or skillful means in getting your goals accomplished but you work with a certain gentle ease. To have a knack is to have something beyond basic skills.

As an entrepreneur, no doubt you can come out on top of your industry because of your hard work, your intelligence, and talents. However, having a knack at doing what you do is something almost abstract and beyond those basic qualities. Really it means you have an innate ease of understanding about what you are doing.

Having a knack may be something you are born with or something you can develop. If you are not born with a knack, for example, the knack to diagnose a car engine, you can still study hard and gain lots of experience, until at some point you have mastered engine diagnosis to the point where you look like you were born with that knack.

In the end, it may look like you have some kind of magical insight and skill. This winning principle applies to whatever business you undertake. Having a knack or developing a knack for what your entrepreneurial efforts are all about gives you an ingenious way of getting to your business goals faster and easier.

Kiosk

It's OK to Start Small!

Every entrepreneur wants to start big and make a big splash. However, you may have a product or service and you need to start small. Renting a small space at a mall or a concert that has a steady flow of traffic without having to spend thousands of dollars on buildout, you might use a kiosk.

Using a kiosk puts you in the company of major retailers, especially if you are at an established and busy mall. A kiosk allows you to be in front of foot traffic which gives you the same and sometimes better exposure than a giant brand retailer. A kiosk is user-friendly and an easy way to get personal with passers-by, building awareness of your brand and building customer relations.

Kiosks have given me the opportunity to better develop my sales pitch, as well as do major business that was completely unexpected. For a minimal investment, I can offer both my goods and services immediately to new customers, even offering a discreet discount to a hesitant buyer.

A word of caution here: Do your research not just on the costs of your kiosk but also on the foot traffic associated with the location of your choice. One successful kiosk may lead to a second one, and you can gain the experience and feedback you need in your new venture economically.

Kindness

A Little Kindness Goes a Long Way!

Despite early childhood hardships, I have been blessed with a good heart that continues to exude kindness. Kindness can be defined as the quality of being friendly, generous, and considerate. I choose this word because I am not seeing enough entrepreneurs who understand how relevant the principle of kindness is to the foundation and the success of your business.

Kindness can and does take you further any day than not being kind. I have known those who have operated on both sides: kind and unkind. The kind, generous, loving, caring, smiling entrepreneur always gets further down the road to success. The unkind entrepreneur is stingy, not caring enough, edgy or nervous, or even devious.

You can do simple acts of kindness by simply being sympathetic to your client's situation or circumstance, and offering a simple and affordable solution to their acquiring your product or service. Hey, I have even accepted IOU's from time to time, and most of the time have gotten my payment. Those who did not keep their payment commitments, I just wrote them off to charity and that made me feel better.

Any time you are giving to others through the kindness of your heart, the Universe or the Divine Intelligence notices and will bless your kindness and grace you with all kinds of positive returns that will surprise you. Plus, your business will grow!

Kickback

Call It a Give-Back!

Get a good understanding of the term kickback. I like to think of it more as a give-back. The familiar term kickback has two distinct meanings; when spelled separately, to kick back means to sit back and chill; when spelled as one word, kickback means to receive a form of payment for something you have done.

Many businesses participate in kickbacks, including credit card companies, hotels, airlines, restaurants, grocery stores, and even some non-profits. They basically offer kickbacks to loyal customers in the form of what are termed reward programs and other incentives. Some kickbacks are legal, and some are illegal.

We read about corporate executives who come under public and legal scrutiny because of kickbacks they receive in awarding one company a contract over another company's business bids. These types of kickbacks are also called bribes.

Non-profits participate in incentives by soliciting in-kind donations, where instead of giving money to a charity to buy needed goods and services, the goods and services themselves are given by a company or individual. The donating party receives a kickback from the government in the form of a tax credit.

Be very clear about what kind of kickback or incentives you are offering to your clients so that it's all above the table.

Key

What is the Key?

You are the key that unlocks the success to your business. You have the key to unlock the storehouse of your personal goods and those of your enterprise. Every decision that you make for your business is key. The keys are in your hands. This is the key point!

As an entrepreneur, you are the key person. At some point in the evolution of your business, you will need another key person to make sure your business systems and personnel are in compliance with whatever goals and regulations you have established for your business.

Within your industry you should be able to identify the key players who are making headlines and forging ahead of you. What makes them key to your industry sector?

Your key to greater success is to find that one particular factor which is central to keeping you moving toward your goal. Search for that key and you will find it!

Keep

You Are the Keeper!

To keep means have or retain possession, to continue or cause to continue in a specified condition, position, or course. As an entrepreneur, you must keep your overall grip on your business. Keep abreast of the sales you make and the sales that you have set as goals. Keep up with what's relevant to the consumer, and in the industry. Keep up with team members' work, noting who needs to be promoted or, conversely, who needs to be dismissed.

Keep tabs of new legislation that affects your industry. Keep yourself in a state of receptivity. Keep things that serve your highest good. Keep your body in the best possible state. Keep your eyes open and your mouth shut at critical times, especially when it is best to observe silence. Keep all your personal devices and business tools operable and equipped with the latest programs.

Keep yourself relevant to the public that your business serves. Keep celebrating those who are working with you. Keep up with your team's spirits and sales. Keep on keepin' on!

Keen

Keep Keen!

To been keen means to have highly developed capacities, to be sharp, to be very focused on something. Entrepreneurs, be keenly aware of what your aspirations are before making your first business move. Being keen gives you an edge on the competition and allows you to make moves in a concentrated way like a professional athlete. Being keen means that you are beyond critical understanding, you see the outcome clearly.

Being keen is a state of mind that you want to develop early on in your entrepreneurial endeavor. Have a keen awareness of the proper timing to launch a product or service. There is a season for everything, and you must be keenly aware of when it is time to make your move. For example, you don't need a keen sense of awareness that toys sell better in December than in July. However, a keen sense of where toy sales are found during the rest of the year will keep your enterprise stable and consistent.

Being keen is almost a sixth sense but it can be developed by a serious entrepreneur through mindfulness practices and maintaining your best intentions.

Karma

It Can Be Your Friend!

As an entrepreneur, be aware of the simple, universal principle of karma. Karma is the sum of one's actions in thought, word and deed. This is also known as the great law of cause and effect. You decide your destiny by understanding and being in congruence with good karma.

There is no escape from karma so your only course of action is to realize the wisdom of being keenly aware of all that you think, say and do unto others. Therefore, as you take account of your business decisions and put them into plans of action, you will actually start to know what to expect from those actions. In other words, starting with pure wholesome intentions, speaking the truth about your wares and acting in accordance with the highest good, your entrepreneurial efforts cannot fail. It's the law!

The law of karma works both for you and against you. It's simply our choice to be law abiding citizens or outlaws. So plan your actions (karmas) accordingly and be mindful every moment of your wholesome thoughts, words and deeds—especially during those tough times that you will certainly encounter in any enterprise.

Monitor your karma continuously so you feel the flow of love, hope, and goodness from where you ultimately derive your business success.

L

Legacy

What Will You Leave Behind?

Take into account what you want your legacy to be in this life. The Latin derivative of the word comes from 'what is delegated.' The definition has come to mean a gift or a bequest that is handed down, endowed or conveyed from one person to another.

If you are a serious entrepreneur, you should know that one great benefit of your position is that you are afforded the opportunity to create a legacy, something that can be passed on to others, including the next generation. Therefore, ask yourself what you want your legacy to be or to look like once you are ready to pass the mantle. Who will you groom to carry out your legacy?

The sooner you start this process, the better you will see what happens after you depart from your business, what kind of successors or heirs you want to leave running the enterprise you worked so hard to create and sustain. What is the human mark you want to leave behind, your epitaph?

Consider that your legacy is one of the most important things for you to take into account going forward as an entrepreneur because it gives you a much larger and more beneficial perspective on your total journey.

Lessons

Life Lessons?

You will learn valuable lessons through your entrepreneurial experience, about yourself, your associates, your community and the whole world of business. If you want to fast-pace your business, do your best to learn from the lessons of others because you or your business might not survive some of the experiences that life pitches at you.

Learning by life lessons is the hardest way to learn. When you hear, "Don't reinvent the wheel," it means learn your lessons, not theoretically nor necessarily through experience but preferably through study and mentorship. I have seen too many entrepreneurs and their enterprises go under unnecessarily because they failed to listen to sage advice from those entrepreneurs who previously faced the same or similar experiences.

If you want to accelerate and move past certain obstacles, learn the lesson from those who had the good fortune to survive the challenging experiences that threatened to destroy them or their business.

Leader

What Makes a Great Leader?

As an entrepreneur, become a leader and think of yourself as a leader, whether you see yourself as one or not. When you take on the role of an entrepreneur you are at the forefront of your business enterprise, and people will be looking up to you for advice and guidance.

This is what leaders do; they guide and forge forward ahead of their constituency, their group, or their organization. As an entrepreneur, you are the one who is responsible for the launch of products and services, for initiating the business. You become the principal player. You must take on the leadership role, understand the capacities required for your ultimate performance, and demonstrate your vision and resolve for your enterprise to succeed.

Study the great leaders—in business, politics, religion, education, medicine, art—so that you are inspired and understand what made them great leaders and emulate the qualities that suit you and your enterprise. The better the leader, the greater his or her chances are for advancement and success. You might be a 'born leader' or not, but either way you still must cultivate your gifts or vision, and learn and practice the necessary steps that create a bona fide leader.

Leadership is about being responsible to yourself, your employees, your customers and community. Knowing how and when to respond to everyday challenges is what takes you to the next level.

There are many books written on successful leaders but it is beyond the scope of this book to go into the many qualities inherent in great leadership. The study of successful leaders and how they became successful will prove beneficial to you.

Location

What Does Location Mean Today?

Of course you have heard the old mantra: location, location, location. The importance of where you locate your business, either in brick and mortar or on the internet, is one of the primary consideration for any entrepreneur. If you are selling a product, what is the location of your manufacturer or your outlet? If you are selling a service or a product, what is the location where one can receive this product or service?

Location is obviously important if you rely on foot traffic for a retail business. Either brick or mortar or internet-based commerce needs SEO (Search Engine Optimization) in order to bring customers to your location. We're not talking just about finding a busy street corner in Manhattan to sell ties, socks and scarves. However, I do know a successful young entrepreneur who sets up a pizza and sodas table outside his local high school every day at 3:00 PM and rakes in a nice ROI selling to hungry kids getting out of school every day.

Increasingly the concept of location is more and more sophisticated. What is the best location for your business office, taking into consideration rents, prestige areas, and convenience for employees, suppliers and customers?

Today, you must get up-to-the-minute info from experts in order to know where and how to best position your product or service. Yes, location is still a big part of your sales and success equation.

Lease

What Are You Agreeing To?

Entrepreneurs, if you are going into brick and mortar, understand your lease terms and conditions. I remember leasing a storefront in San Diego, California a few years ago for my jewelry business. Every year for the four years that I rented my storefront, the property manager came to me and wanted to secure an additional security deposit for the storefront. I had never agreed to this requirement in the original lease. Unbeknownst to me, the original owner had sold the building shortly after I moved in and the 'property manager' was actually the new owner who decided to change my original lease agreement.

This would not have taken me by surprise if I had thoroughly read my original lease agreement which spelled out the changes that could occur under various circumstances, such as a new owner coming in and changing the original lease. Leases are tricky, whether you are leasing a car or kiosk in a shopping mall. Pay careful attention to the language in any agreement—rental leases, employee contracts, consignment agreements or subscriptions—so that you understand everything you are signing up for and that you do not have any unpleasant surprises down the road.

Liability

Understand Your Responsibilities

Liability is defined as the state of being responsible for something, especially by law; or a person or thing whose presence or behavior is likely to cause embarrassment or put one at a disadvantage. Every entrepreneur will confront a liability at some point in their career. You need to know how to handle this challenge when you are confronted by a liability to your enterprise.

First, you are responsible for your employees' conduct. If their behavior becomes a disadvantage to your business, you have to make them aware of it and inform them of the type of conduct that they should be displaying at all times. If an employee steps out of line with a customer by not following your rules, you may have to pay for that through a lawsuit or settlement. Your liability will come in the form of a financial compensation that your insurance company may cover, or that they may not cover.

Know what you need to know in order to shield yourself and your business from any liability; business, personal or property. Check out the proper insurance coverage for your property and goods that is standard in your business. Do your comparative insurance shopping to cover your liabilities but don't try to save money by getting policies that do not fully cover every contingency.

As an entrepreneur of course you are a risk taker but you must always look to protect yourself in case a disaster occurs, whether from natural causes, such as a flood or earthquake, or from mistakes made by you or your team, or a product defect, or some negligence regarding your physical business property.

And remember, a problem that involves liability can negatively affect the goodwill that you have built up in your business which will also cost you. In simple terms, cover your butt!

Land

Real estate is real!

Entrepreneurs, I recommend purchasing the land where your brick and mortar business is located. When I opened my first brick and mortar store, my landlord asked me if I wanted to buy the building and another one on the same block. I was comfortable with leasing and fearful of buying.

Consequently, the real estate market shifted, and my landlord sold the building. When the new owner came in, they raised the rent so high that it was out of my range. To add insult to injury, they offered to sell the buildings to me for a million dollars—a lot more than my original landlord offered the land to me.

My hesitation at accepting the second offer did not work out well either. The second owner's price turned out to be a good price, considering that twenty years later the properties are now valued at twenty million dollars. I still regret that I was so fearful and insecure that I did not buy that property.

Owning the land on which your physical business is a win-win situation, especially if your business is doing well. If you have an offer to take a physical stake in a property and you have a vision about how to make good business use of that land, investigate the offer with a real estate professional and make an effort to grab the land and use it wisely.

Labor

Make it a Labor of Love!

As an entrepreneur, you must be willing to labor if you want to get results. Labor is typically defined as hard work performed with difficulty. Being an entrepreneur is hard work, no doubt about it.

Therefore, let your labor be one of love and excellence. That means that you have started your entrepreneurial enterprise for the highest good, not just for material or personal purposes but for a spiritual and uplifting purpose, whatever your product or service is. You never want to feel like you are laboring in vain. In our church, there is a hymn we sing, "Lest you built a house for the Lord, you labor in vain." As entrepreneurs, we should aspire to perfect our offerings and to effectively labor to achieve our grandest vision.

You and your team are laboring to create an excellent product from a mindset of excellence. Sure, sometimes your efforts feel like labor, days when you feel like you are slogging through a difficult landscape. Remember, especially on those days, that your labor is for a very worthwhile cause and that you will reach the Promised Land.

Lawyer

Mitigate Risk!

As an entrepreneur, you are that person who is willing to take a risk. Therefore, you need to fortify yourself against surprise or even calamitous risk. I strongly suggest that you find and keep several lawyers, either as friends or on retainer.

Lawyers get a bad rap but you need to understand their function and value. I have yet to encounter an entrepreneur who has not at some juncture needed a lawyer. The great state of California, where I lived for many years, has the reputation of being the most litigious state in the nation. In California, people are always being confronted with some form of lawsuit. What brings about these lawsuits?

You might have a disagreement with a business partner, or you might have to confront someone legally in order to collect a debt, or fight an injustice. It is better to have a lawyer to call and not need their services, than to need the services of a lawyer and not have one you know and trust. To help you launch your enterprise and to help keep you on course, I highly recommend that you investigate legal counsel even before you need it. And I will add here, with great respect, how thankful I am for how much I have learned about the law and legal procedures from my lawyers as friends and necessary business associates.

Law

Know the Law!

Entrepreneurs, I can tell you that if you start out with an understanding of the laws that govern life and the city, state, and country in which you reside, you will understand how to better and faster grow your business.

When I first started selling jewelry I would sell it at various church venues. Then I started selling to the broader public without even knowing that I needed a business license. As my business grew, I wanted to reach more people and make more money, so I went to selling on the city streets. To my surprise, someone called the police on me. The caller stated that I had stolen all the jewelry. The police approached me at my street location, questioned me, then handcuffed and drove me to jail. I was able to prove that I bought the merchandise and that it was only costume jewelry. I was just fourteen years old at the time, and the whole ordeal was very scary. But that experience woke me up concerning the law.

I obtained a business license and a seller's permit which gave me the latitude that I needed to work within the law. Remember that not knowing the law is no excuse to a magistrate. You will still face a stiff fine or worse when you do something illegal consciously or out of ignorance. You do not want to learn the laws of your city or state through experience.

Consult with other professionals in your industry, do the internet research, make the phone calls you need to the city and state agencies in order to get the information you need to be a law-abiding and successful business person.

M

Momentum

Just Keep It Moving!

Momentum is defined as the impetus gained by a moving object. There will be times during the course of your enterprise when things are slow so the concept of momentum is that you keep going even when you have no visible wind in your sails. As an entrepreneur, once you have started out the gate, gaining momentum is important to remaining relevant to your core clients and new ones.

One way to keep momentum going is to have consistently greater goals. Keep up your momentum through advertising, word of mouth, and the many social media outlets available today. Learn guerilla marketing which is defined as innovative, unconventional, and low-cost marketing techniques aimed at obtaining maximum exposure for a product. You can offer classes and seminars to educate the public on your product or services. Learn to use the media in print, radio and television, including talk shows and infomercials, to let the public know about your product or service.

The internet provides many ways to keep the momentum going too, such as blogging. Sales and giveaways are also fantastic ways to keep up the momentum. Charity events and fund-raising through partnerships and affiliations help keep momentum going.

The more creative ways that you discover to activate your momentum and keep it going, the greater your chances for finding new and sometimes surprising business opportunities.

Mission

Know Your Mission!

As an entrepreneur, you have embarked on a mission in life. Your mission should be fully disclosed for all to see. Make it a part of your business plan and see that all of your employees and team members understand that you are not in business just to make money but that you are on a mission to make a difference.

Your mission in life is, and should be, in sync with your purpose which is fundamentally to be a beneficial presence on this planet. You are here to shine your light. Serving the greater good for humanity makes for a solid entrepreneurial foundation and mission. Have a business mission statement on your website and in all of your promotions.

Think of your life and your mission in business as one and the same. Money motives of course are important but without an intentional and spiritual understanding of what each of us is really doing here individually and collectively, life may get to be empty even if you achieve wealth and material goods. Your mission is a gift from the Creator and as I have aligned myself with this philosophy over the years, I have seen business success beyond my wildest imagination—and you will too!

Merge

Mergers and Their Benefits

No doubt you have heard about big Wall Street corporations merging or one corporation acquiring a competitor or a business that furthers its own long term goals. As an entrepreneur maybe at an opportune time you should consider merging your business with a friend who has a business, resources or skills that you do not have and that you do not want to build up yourself.

Merge in a way that is beneficial and viable for everyone involved. Do your due diligence in any business or personal merger. When forming a merger, you will want to consult with your legal team, your accountant, or an outside consultant.

A smart and timely merger can assure the survival of your businesses at a critical moment, or make you and your new partner stronger in the midst of stiff competition or a business downturn. Merger can be an alternative to going out of business. And don't let your ego get in the way if you need to merge in order to survive.

Market

Understanding Markets

Your market is literally where you sell your product or services. Someone who sells vegetables will be found at a farmer's market, not at an electronics show. As an entrepreneur, identify the buyers in your market and strategize how best to reach them in your market, especially if you are in a very competitive market.

Find the right sales staff who understands your market and can skillfully sell to your targeted customers in that market, whether you are selling a service or product. If you are selling to millennials, it makes sense to have some enthusiastic millennials on your sales staff. If you manufacture a product, you have to investigate wholesale and retail market prices for that product.

To make a profit in your market, perhaps you have to manufacture overseas and not in the US. If your product or service is being marketed in a foreign country, you must understand the tariffs that come with bringing products into that country. The laws and taxes must be understood thoroughly both here and in foreign markets so that there are no unpleasant surprises. Understand the importance your bank's letters of credit in doing business in foreign markets. Imports and exports require a knowledge of currency exchange rates, shipping, customs regulations, fees, duties and bonds.

Be aware of what is legally permitted for distribution in your market. It is very important to have local connections in both the manufacturing country and the country to which they are being imported. Also, it is wise to have your network of distributors in place before you order a large product purchase. Calculating the wholesale or retail prices for your product in your market and still making a profit after expenses is obviously important too. Once you have done all this groundwork, keep your eyes and ears open as you enter and do business in your market.

Mascot

Get a Mascot!

As an entrepreneur, you carry your brand with you everywhere you go. People are looking at you to see what your brand stands for, so if you are in the service business—and we all are whether or not we realize it—there might be a point at which you will want to use a mascot.

Traditionally, a mascot is defined as a person, animal, or object adopted by a group or organization as a symbolic figure, especially to bring them good luck. Commercially, mascots attract customers and burnish an image in the public mind about your brand. Think of the gecko lizard in the GEICO Insurance ads, or the duck in the Aflac ads, or the global Ronald McDonald.

A mascot is a fun and easy way to remember your product or service. Young kids especially love mascot characters. If kids and moms and grandmas are your target market, get a professional graphic artist to help you create a cute mascot early in your business enterprise. Take your mascot with you on all sales calls and promotions. You can get a plush mascot toy manufactured inexpensively. Your mascot is a part of your team, and may become a very important part of your team.

Motive

What Are You Doing It For?

You must ask yourself what your motive is for becoming an entrepreneur, a true risk-taker. Your motive should be connected to what inspires you to begin your enterprise and to continue in spite of the obstacles that will eventually show up.

Your motive must give you the will power to conquer every seeming challenge. Motives that are regulated by passion and purpose get the necessary fuel that allows you to recharge when you have been depleted of energy. Allow your motives to be good ones.

I know that money is important, and I highly recommend that you let earning money be a motivating factor. However, money can't be the only motivating factor. Being motivated by what you like, or better still, by what you love and what you truly enjoy doing will more easily produce the financial returns you seek. You can also be motivated by the knowledge that what you are doing will make you an upstanding citizen who is doing his or her part to make the world a better place.

Sure, you must help yourself first, then your family and friends, then your spiritual community, and next your collective community. The pattern of helping yourself in order to help others is ultimately the best motive to foster your total personal and business success.

Mandatory

What Ya Gotta Do!

Every entrepreneur soon discovers that there are certain things that they must do in order to ensure that their business is a success. It's mandatory to take the first step. I know that seems obvious but how many people have we met who have great ideas but never step up to the plate?

First, take action once you determine that you have a passion or knack for doing something for which you would like to be paid. Go for it! If you don't go for it, somebody else surely will, especially once your ideas mysteriously get out on the psychic airwaves. It's mandatory that you know, meaning that you have the confidence that somehow or some way, there will come a mysterious or surprising support for whatever you decide to do with your precious life. Just as you embark on a plane or a ship, of course you know where the life vests are but you anyway climb happily on board.

Second, and this is an imperative, it is mandatory that you are willing and prepared to take a fall now and then in the form of a mistake in judgement, a miscommunication, bad timing or a force majeure. (And it's mandatory to expand your vocabulary!) It's mandatory to learn the mantra: So what? Now what? It's mandatory as an entrepreneur that you get up, brush yourself off, and do it all over again—as many times as you get tripped up. Life is about learning, so if you do fall, then you know not to fall that way again.

Third, it's mandatory to get rid of the shame and blame game. Know that the buck stops right at your desk. That means that you do not have time to sit around and blame others for your mistakes. It's mandatory not to waste time and energy in self-punishment. Get over it, get over yourself and continue to press toward your higher calling and purpose. To summarize, these three things are mandatory: (1) Take action, (2) Get back up when you fall down, and (3) Avoid shame and blame.

Magnetize

How to Draw It to You!

An entrepreneur should know how to create such a presence in the marketplace that people are magnetized by you, and your product or service. To be magnetized means to be strongly attracted to something or someone. The best possible way to do this is to start by developing a superior quality product and/or superior service.

Once you do this, go out in brag about what you got going in your own cool and magnetic way. I don't mean that you need to thump your chest but you should make truthful claims in superlative terms through all the various types of media available. When people try and love your product or service and because you magnetized them with some dazzling sales presentation, they will become your magnets in the form of positive social media reviews and old fashioned word of mouth. Word of mouth is still a very powerful advertising and marketing tool, and with social media, people can send rave reviews to thousands of people with just one click of their cursor. And remember that people do pay attention to other people's views and reviews.

Therefore, be mindful of the creative ways in which you can magnetize your business and draw customers to your door or your website.

Maintain

Show You Care!

The verb 'to maintain' means to cause or enable a condition or state of affairs to continue. When you maintain something, even a potted plant, it means that you care about that something. As an entrepreneur, I am mindful, and I maintain mindfulness. I want you also to be mindful and maintain mindfulness.

Maintain your personal relationships. If you have a life's companion and family, set aside ample time to maintain your caring relationship with them for the ultimate flourishing of your tribe. Too many entrepreneurs make the mistake of focusing on the business and money to the extent that they forget about the importance of maintaining their personal relationship with family, friends and their community. Find a way to maintain a balance between your enterprise and your personal relationships.

Maintain a good relationship with your body too by exercising, eating right and getting enough sleep. Maintain a good relationship with your soul and your Creator through your meditation practice, prayer, visioning and charity work. The maintenance of these important relationships will help you in your daily business life, as well as when the hard times hit you and your business. Don't neglect this the important entrepreneurial principle of maintenance as it applies from every physical detail of your business, even as minute as you the boss picking up some unseen litter from your premise to the largest parts of your business.

And again, I stress the ultimate importance of maintaining the best personal relationships you can for your ultimate success as an entrepreneur and in being a beneficial presence on the planet.

Mentor

Know Someone Who Knows!

As an entrepreneur, you are wise when you find a mentor for yourself. Most successful entrepreneurs have or have had that special teacher or guide to teach them about operating a business.

A mentor can help you avoid making unnecessary mistakes, and can even prevent your business from experiencing a major disaster. Confucius, the classic Chinese sage, said that there are three ways to learn: experience, meditation, and imitation. He said that experience is the worst way to learn, and that imitation is the best way to learn. Find a trusted mentor and follow what they tell you.

Find that special person who is willing to give of their time and knowledge, and be happy to give something of value back in return for their wisdom, expertise and time. Don't fight with your mentor, even if they tell you something that is painful to hear.

Honor your mentor, even before and especially after you see their words and vision were correct in aiding the success of your enterprise. Having a real mentor throughout your entrepreneurial life is a real blessing!

N

New

What So New About It?

Know that all things become new but that nothing is actually new. I know that sounds like a contradiction but what I am saying is that what's new is usually only a new way of doing something. If you look at all of the hamburger joints near you, you will notice nothing new about the basic hamburger itself. It's just made in a different fashion by each business. There's nothing new about chicken, except that different franchises make it differently. The same is true of pizza, tacos, the neighborhood dry cleaners or bank.

Concepts and fashions are what constitute change and get billed as being new but the basic items themselves are often the same sure thing. So, figure out what is truly new about your enterprise. Nobody wants the same old-same old that is obviously thinly disguised from the one down the block, or in the same internet search category.

Remember that new should mean unique, original, not seen before, gotta try it! Really take the time to figure out what separates your new product or service from your competitors. People want to try something new, see something new, experience something new. Don't you?

And remember, your new thing is not only new but the way you present it, your promotions and advertisements, should be new too. Novelty attracts attention, whether it is depicted in a sophisticated or goofy manner is part of your success in attracting attention to your new product or service. And again, what gets a customer curious is the new thing that is actually new and different, and most importantly, better than the old thing.

Now

Don't Wander!

As an entrepreneur, you must be willing to stay in the now because now is all there is. The past is gone, leave it behind. Don't bother to look in your rear view mirror too much because as the famous baseball pitcher Satchel Paige said, "They're comin' up right behind you." Even the future is a part of the now because we determine our future by our actions in the now.

Keeping in the now means to remain vigilant and mindful of what is happening in the present. When you get skilled at being very alert in the now, you will start to make better choices and decisions for the success of your business. If you are not in the now, it means you are somewhere else in your head and you may not notice what is directly in front of you.

Being committed to taking the necessary actions for your enterprise that will bring about the desired future demands that you remain in the now. When you watch athletes compete, you notice that they have the basic skills, as well as inner grit but the truly great athletes are somehow even more in the present than their competitors, meaning that they see a bigger picture than the opposing players. Allow the present moment to help you overcome any obstacles or hindrances that might block your progress into your now moment of entrepreneurial greatness.

Never

The Power of Never!

As a true entrepreneur, you never lose sight of your goals and dreams. In order for you to be a phenomenal success, you must never move forward without possessing a clear plan of action. Knowing what your plan of action is will help you to steer clear of hindrances and obstacles that never fail to try and sidetrack you from reaching your desired goals.

Of course, as an entrepreneur, you learn to never say never because the word impossible is not in your vocabulary. I trust that whatever you can clearly conceive, you can clearly achieve and reach your dream. I can never believe otherwise.

As Henry Ford famously said, "If you think you can, or you think you can't, you're right." Never believe you can't. Remember, you must be part of the entrepreneurial tribe of can-do people. Never listen to or believe those naysayers who are telling you that you can't do this or that.

Never stop focusing on your dream, knowing that energy flows where your intention and attention goes. As the saying goes, keep your eye on your prize. Never give up!

No

Know Your Boundaries!

Successful entrepreneurs know what they want and what they don't want, what's good for business and what is not good for business. Both the power of Yes! and the power of No! are powerful tools for an entrepreneur to use. Learn to use your mystical third eye that discriminates between what is wholesome and what is not wholesome for you, your employees, your business and your future.

For many people, saying No is difficult. You want to be polite and not hurt another person's feelings. That's natural. But you have to know when and how to use the power of No. Believe me, you will certainly meet some expert salespeople trying to sell you an attractive product or service for your business. Look at the salesperson as closely as you look at the goods they are offering you.

And yes, you will meet some crooks along your entrepreneurial path, as well an incompetent persons who do not deserve your time, energy or dollars. Yes, it even gets personal as when people have asked me for money and other things just because they knew that I had it. This has taught me to develop the important capacity to say No.

This capacity to say No can be crucial to your personal and business survival. And ultimately, saying an appropriate and timely No is better than lying or pretending that you don't have what you are being asked for by a person, family member, team member or a customer. I am not saying to be cruel or unkind but know how and when to use your third eye and know when it just makes plain sense to say No.

One of my mottos is, "Why tell a lie when the truth will do?" Don't be afraid of the word No. Take your feelings out of it. I have asked people for things and they've said Yes. Later they never followed through and of course this did not sit well with me, and sabotaged our relationship. I wish they had told me No rather than to blatantly lie to me.

Never be afraid of a person or an organization that you allow them to hold so much power over you that you feel you must lie instead of just saying No when it's necessary to do so. That person may not like you for saying No but they will certainly respect you. No can be your friend!

Nourish

Take Care of Numero Uno Too!

The importance of nourishing yourself to supply yourself with whatever promotes your own growth and development has to be stated here. Entrepreneurs can easily forget about themselves. You have to continually feed your mind and body with the proper nutrients, vitamins, minerals and other essentials that will give you the fuel necessary to be mentally, physically, and spiritually healthy.

You may find yourself caught up so much in the swing of things going on and around your business enterprise that you neglect to properly nourish your body Remember to exercise, eat well and drink plenty of fluids. Don't skip breakfast, lunch or dinner.

Remember to nourish your family and friends and your personal community, the very things that are integral to your success by giving them the proper, respectful and timely attention when it is required of you.

Nourish your mind by reading an inspiring book every day. Nourish your soul with meditation and affirmative prayer, communing with the Creator either on your own or in a community setting, doing some charity work (and not just writing a check). Go out and commune with nature by taking a hike or walk along the ocean or a lake. Turn off your phone for a while during the daytime. Find and maintain a beautiful, intimate and loving relationship with someone.

Remember the mantra: Nourish, and you will flourish!

Niche

Know Your Niche!

In business, a niche is defined as denoting or relating to products, services, or interests that appeal to a small, specialized section of the population. The faster an entrepreneur finds their niche, the faster you get laser-targeted and better at what you offer to your segment of the market.

Find your niche by knowing what you like to do and what you can do well is a key to success. All entrepreneurs find their niche. Develop a method to monetize that niche, stay focused and true to your core niche and you will experience an exponential rise in energy and wealth. I have found this to be the ideal method to help focus on success.

And remember, an entrepreneur knows when they have found their niche because it proves to be not only financially viable but also makes their heart glad while simultaneously inspiring and helping their employees, family, community and the public at large.

Network

Network, Network, Network!

The entrepreneur's network—that is, their expanded channels of communications, client base, manufacturing or service providers, shipping logistics, internet savvy, industry leaders and industry associations—will oftentimes determine an entrepreneur's success and ultimately their net worth.

Networking is crucial, and knowing how to network with key people is a valuable skill for every entrepreneur to learn in order to grow their business. Networking is about more than just showing up at functions, introducing yourself, handing out your business card and only being interested in promoting your business interests. Effective networking is also about connecting with other people, being genuinely interested in what they do, even if it is not directly connected to what your business is about. Being a warm and connected human being brings rewards onto itself, as well as down the road some surprise introduction or connection may come your way through that initial human interaction.

When you approach networking this way, the laws that govern the Universe will send someone that you need to meet in your direction to help you. This person will like what you are doing and will understand the good that can come from it, and will benefit your venture in some important way. This kind synergy is what constitutes effective networking. The result of this kind of networking will be that your business will flourish by moving forward in a more integrated way.

Negotiation

Learn The Art of Negotiation!

An entrepreneur must learn the art of negotiation. The quicker you learn this art—and it is an imperfect, intangible art, more than a skill—the faster and further you will go in the development of your enterprise. At every phase of your business you will have to negotiate with investors, partners, employees, suppliers, even your maintenance crew. And when you get home, you'll have to negotiate with your wife and kids!

The true art of negotiation, as the legendary negotiator Herb Cohen said, is to create a win-win compromise. You get some of what you want and the people on the other side of the table get some of what they want. The goal is that when all the parties leave the negotiation, even if they are not completely happy, still they still remain in business together because of their mutual needs. Effective negotiating is about creating a beneficial outcome for everyone involved.

Most university MBA programs surprisingly don't teach negotiation as it is not a science like macro-economics. There are many books written on negotiation techniques. I recommend Herb Cohen's book You Can Negotiate Anything. Another recommendation: Never Split the Difference by Chris Voss.

One of the basic techniques is to keep emotions out of the negotiation process. Another important point to remember in negotiation is that any party can at any time get up from the table and walk away. What are you willing to pay or do for what the other guy has that you want? What won't you do or pay?

Then, how will you get what you want, while helping them get what they want? This super-important tool of negotiation can make or break your business as you are bargaining for serious needs that ultimately affect the success of your business. When athletes and owners negotiate, or when unions and management negotiate, when national governments negotiate— they are entering into a real cauldron for high stakes results that many times involve even life and death issues. Please study and work on how to come up with negotiated solutions that benefit everyone.

Necessary

Details, Large and Small

Entrepreneurs, sooner or later, you will discover that there are going to be times when something essential and necessary needs to occur in your business. What is necessary for your business should not come as a surprise because you are sticking close to your mission and its execution. However, surprises obviously do occur in life and business, so be open and available to do the necessary things when called upon to do them on short notice.

It's necessary for every entrepreneur to be agile, to be able to stop or turn on a dime, to know when it's time to pivot, dodge, jump, stand still or just plain back up. Sometimes we get caught up in the hustle and flow of making money and forget the small things that are necessary for our business success.

The old saying applies here: "How you do anything is how you do everything." When you miss a small, necessary thing like saying 'thank you' to a customer, or not showing your appreciation for their patronage, that can cause some small hurt feelings which may be remembered by the customer. I find it necessary to be particularly vigilant about the small things.

Also, it is necessary to give recognition and praise for the accomplishments of your team members, employees and associates. Everyone likes to feel needed and appreciated. Don't you? Staying in contact with family and friends who support your endeavors, and thanking them is necessary too. These personal touches are just as necessary as your major and minor daily business concerns.

It's necessary to keep an eagle eye on how employees are performing their duties. Sometimes it's necessary to relieve a certain team member from those duties so they can be free to innovate in other areas of your business empire. It's necessary to stay abreast of major and minor trends or changes in your industry. It's necessary to know what can possibly interfere with your enterprise's progress, preferably before those interferences and disruptions occur. Pay attention to what's necessary all around you, large and small.

Natural

Be True to Yourself!

An entrepreneur must do and say what is natural for them. That does not mean you should be impolite or crude, or in old hippie terms, "Just let it hang out." There are times when entrepreneurs get overwhelmed by everything they are trying to accomplish and they lose their natural inner joy or their outer happy demeanor.

What is natural for entrepreneurs is to convey enthusiasm for their offering and for the fire of their innately-endowed gifts. If you lose that excitement for a moment, you may try to cover up your temporary disappointment or frustration in some unnatural way. Don't forget that besides your words, people read your tones, gestures and body language. If you feel yourself lose your natural cheerful self for a short while—which is actually natural now and then—just tell your team that you need to take a break. Then do something natural, like going out for a walk around the block and taking a few conscious breaths.

Trying to do what is unnatural for you is the same as going against the grain, and it will make for a harder journey. Remember the pure intentions you began with in establishing your entrepreneurial venture. The Universe will support you by providing natural resources for you to continue your passage in natural joy.

To be natural is at the core of your life's essence because it means to be in alignment and harmony with your original God-given nature. When you allow your natural self to take shape or to be reshaped, your business and personal travels become more enjoyable and easier to navigate toward your goals. Do what is natural in this conscious manner and watch the doors of the Universe fling wide open, allowing you and your business to blossom naturally, just like a beautiful flower in its due season.

O

Outline

See the Outline of Your Business!

As an entrepreneur, it behooves you to create an outline of what you want to accomplish with your business. Identify each of your topics with headers, then sub-headers. Figure out your main points and then create and arrange your main points, as well as your sub-points in a logical way so any employee or team member can easily follow what you have determined is vital to your enterprise.

Remember, an outline is a vital part of your business plan. It gives you an easy, visible format to view the necessary structure or blueprint for your endeavors. However, the outline does not have to be fixed or permanent. Once things start moving, you might encounter some necessary changes, so make and keep a template of the outline and remain open and flexible to changes that you might have to make down the road.

Keep your outline and refer to it periodically, maybe even post it to remind your team of your goals and methods to achieve those goals. The outline will remind you of the direction and flow that your business should take, as well as help to monitor your business growth.

Observe

Develop Your Powers of Observation!

An entrepreneur must observe all the different facets of their business. The more you observe, the more insight you gain into what needs to be done to make your business more successful. You definitely want to observe your sales, your capital expenditures, and the distribution of your product. Also observe your customers purchasing patterns, whether cash, credit or other methods are being used by them.

Observe online vs. instore sales so you know where to best expend your promotions and advertising budget. Observe your team members, too. Are they doing their jobs? Observe your industry trends. Developing the entrepreneur's observation skills is highly important. My own pastor says, "Are you describing what you see, or seeing what you describe?" Think about that one.

It means that we have to be truly present to observe what is going on or we are merely projecting our illusions or biases. Learning to stop, step back and coolly survey the general picture or the specifics does take some practice. Learn the skills of real observation as early as possible in your entrepreneurial career.

Ownership

The Pros and Cons

Ownership is important and the establishment of your ownership must be documented, For example, in the arts, whether it's in the music business, in writing or photography, it's best to retain copyright ownership of all of your original work. Trademarks, tradenames and patents are needed to protect your intellectual property and for you to be compensated for the use or licensing of your product.

All of the information to register your ownership is online through various government websites. If you want to use the Smurfs for the packaging of your brand of cookies, you'll have to pay a licensing fee to Studio Peyo in the UK.

Do you lease or own? That is a perennial question in business. Will you own or lease your offices, your equipment, your vehicles? In any enterprise you will have to make those decisions based on your short or long term goals and finances.

As mentioned previously, I should have bought the building and land that my store was located on but to my detriment I didn't purchase when I had the opportunity. Owning can add value to your overall portfolio but it can also be a liability.

Sorry, but there are no clear cut answers to ownership so really study every ownership offer closely to accurately judge, as best as possible, the pros and cons of an ownership opportunity.

Organize

Get All Your Ducks in a Row!

You the entrepreneur are solely responsible for how your organization is organized. To organize means to establish an internal order to the shape, contents and flow of your business system from top to bottom. Each team player needs to have their roles and responsibilities initially organized by you. Being very clear about people's functions within the structure of your organization and you will achieve the necessary results.

The clearer you are, the faster and smoother your organization will achieve its goals. Organize your sales and marketing teams, e-commerce, social media, and the tasks of your CEO, CFO, and COO. With good organization, your management team will be able to bring a greater understanding of the needs and goals of your various operations to the employees in all your divisions.

Create an organization chart in order to help identify and describe the various responsibilities of your departments and their team members. Keep checking that your business stays organized. One small widget in the system that goes off assignment can cause havoc throughout the system. Good organization eliminates confusion, duplication or neglect. Get organized and stay organized!

Option

Know Your Options!

An entrepreneur will master the inner workings of knowing when to exercise options; that is, choices and alternatives. You will be afforded many options as you move forward in the world of entrepreneurship, so you will need to keep your options open to get the best results for your business.

Options may open up for expanding or selling your business, for taking on new partners, for bringing in outside investors by putting out an IPO, or for providing an incentive-shares program for your employees.

Keeping options open can take some courage if, for example, your business is going through a downturn and you need a loan but don't like the terms a lender presents to you. How long can you keep other options open? How creative can you get in seeing other options if you feel backed up against the wall? What options can render the greatest potential outcome for your business?

Entrepreneurs can see what others can't, and that includes options. Understand the freedom and creativity in appreciating the many dimensions of options.

Offer

What's the Real Offer?

What do you have to offer to your buyers and clients? Know precisely what you offer and be able to effectively communicate your offering, not just to your database but also to your employees and community.

Know when it is time to offer sales on seasonal items, or when it is time to offer the right discount price, and when it's time to move older inventory. If you are offered the chance to acquire a business that compliments yours, or some new materials that will be used in manufacturing your product, or a needed service from an outside provider, you will need to know how to offer the right price or appropriate percentage to acquire that offering.

What is so special about your offer to investors? You must be able to calculate all offers with your third eye, the faculty of deep insight and foresight. Over the years of my many entrepreneurial ventures, I have seen numerous winners and losers. Those who didn't factor in and evaluate all the necessary elements of a tempting offer put in front of them sometimes had regrets after the deal, which is also known as 'buyer's remorse.' Conversely, your offers to others must be really well-thought out for maximum and long term benefits.

And again, those offers that come to you must be thoroughly evaluated in a rational, comprehensive and calm manner.

Orders

Make Order of Orders

Orders are what keeps a business afloat. There will always be orders to place and orders to receive, particularly in product sales. Knowing how and when to do both—to place and fulfill orders—is vital to the success of your business. For example, if you have a seasonal business, such as the Christmas holiday product, you must start to place orders to your supplier or manufacturer in the springtime so your product arrives in plenty of time for you to check if there are problems with your incoming order, to set up your promotions, and be sure your fulfillment processes are faultless.

In other words, leave time for mistakes, oftentimes called "a margin of error." Knowing how and when to order will also get you better deals, and will keep you and your team from being unduly stressed and rushed when the orders start to come in, or if a flood of unexpected orders come in. Don't forget that stress is a killer, personally and in business.

Have your fulfillment processes in order from intake to processing to packaging to shipping. Imagine the logistics of Amazon, the biggest order-fulfillment company in the world. Their order fulfillment processes have to be completely streamlined and efficient. Making order of your order-making process, from making orders to fulfilling them with expert competency is imperative!

Obligation

Obligations Are Serious!

As an entrepreneur, you will find that sometimes you need to obligate yourself to someone who is capable of performing a specific task. Know that as you do this, you are still the one who is liable and responsible for the overall output of your product or service. On the positive side, however, an obligation to someone can be the ticket that gets you to your destination.

Sometimes that go-to person to who you obligated responsibilities creates a credible reputation for your business that can either make or break you in the business world. Both you and your chosen most-trusted one must live up to your obligations. In the same way, you have obligations to yourself, your partners, investors, family and friends, and your community-at-large.

If you encounter a situation in which you feel you are not able to hold true to your obligations, never leave your customers or business associate out on a limb. Instead, notify those who are counting on you before they notify you! This is important because even if you are not able to keep your obligations, at least people will cut you some slack because your were forthright early on.

Let your team, customers and those who acknowledge you as their chief know what is going on in plenty of time. Then, as soon as possible, rectify the situation. Remember that even with the best of planning, circumstances and situations occur that may not be directly your fault. You are a fallible human being. You forgive yourself or anyone else who may have contributed to the problem by not fulfilling their obligation, then move on quickly to do the right thing. Do not waste time. The saying here goes, So what? Now what? Be a problem solver, not a blamer. Take the proper steps to acknowledge and resolve the problem, and your credibility as one who fulfills their obligations will remain intact.

Obtain

Obtain It All!

Every entrepreneur has the right to obtain their heart's desire and see their dream come true. Know that it all happens in due season. I say, "in due season" because there will be some dues that you must pay before you reach your goal. Your goal is a destination to which you must steer yourself and your team. You are the captain in the wheelhouse of your enterprise steering your ship to the Port of Expectations Exceeded!

You will obtain all that you set out to obtain. There cannot be any other thought in your mind and heart. Entrepreneurs, including myself, have run out of energy or resources from time to time. If you find yourself in some dire predicament, reaffirm your mission goals, revisit your purest intentions in starting out on the journey. Stay committed! Obtain some more fuel in whatever form you need from finances, personnel, consultation and don't forget to seek a sign, some encouragement from the Universe.

Stick to your original mission and keep the faith, and ye shall obtain the rewards of faith and hard work! You will obtain success. There cannot be any other way.

Original

You Are An Original!

An entrepreneur thinks and operates as an original. The Universe only creates originals, in every species. Every being on this planet is an original. There are no repeats and there will never be another you. The difference between an entrepreneur and a salary worker is that the entrepreneur insists on expressing his originality and getting paid for it.

The faster you embrace your originality, the sooner you can break free of trying to find safety in the herd, where most people reside. That is not a put-down. It is simply our mammalian nature to gather together, to think together, to feed together, to migrate and congregate together.

An entrepreneur is certainly not a loner but an entrepreneur likes to be outside the norm, outside of conventions, to be like nobody else. You have probably heard the expression outlier which is an expression for a person differing from all other members of a particular group or set. Embracing your uniqueness will set you free from the bondage of just coping day-to-day.

Great athletes, great artists, great social workers, great teachers and doctors, and of course, the wealthiest businesspeople, all embrace their greatness as they express their mission through their originality. Each one of us can pause and discover what makes us unique as a true original.

Love and embrace your originality, take some brave steps in the direction of your original self, and watch how phenomenally your product or service is embraced by the public. An original always gets people's attention. Get in sync with your original self!

P

Programs

Your Business Platform

In the past, entrepreneurs were often pictured as some kind of wild breed, not really well-grounded. Software programs and apps are the way a true entrepreneur gets grounded in today's high tech information age. Find and buy a program that works for your product or service to keep track of your client database, manufacturing numbers and prices, inventory, service providers and their performance, sales, employee salaries, bookkeeping for tax purposes and all the other components of your flourishing and expanding business that need to be monitored over the long term.

If you see yourself as the CCO (Chief Creative Officer) and don't like to do the physical or mental part of keeping track of every corner of your business empire, that's OK. Hire someone who loves that wonky and nerdy but necessary component. Let them gather the info, then you review it and make decisions based on what your program numbers and trends tell you, along with the advice of your CPA, your operations manager and your regional sales manager.

Business programs are your friends, even if you don't like the job of gathering the details. Numerous software companies have developed programs to assist small businesses with these matters, so make use of these programs to help things run smoothly for your business. All of these business programs can be found online. You can also hire an outside business software consultant to help you find the right programs for your business and industry sector. This is part of your operations manager's job; that is, to get the right programs for your business and hire the right person to efficiently run the programs. Get with the program!

Power

Connect With It!

An entrepreneur instinctively knows that the power invested within them is to be used for the benefit of all and not wasted. You were born to share your gifts and talents with the world. Learn what you do well, and trust that it is a part of your power that must be turned loose for you and your enterprise to become a beneficial presence on this planet.

This positive power gives you the authority to offer your talents at the highest performance capacity. Your power is that vigor and vitality that moves you in the right direction of your dreams and aspirations. The Creator imbues this power within all of us. Use your God-given power of goodness and wholeness, along with your clever self, to attract people who will assist you in your entrepreneurial enterprise.

Your power asserts a certain confidence and authority that when exerted properly will be felt by your clients and team members, emboldening them to follow your leadership. Notice the swagger of certain great athletes, or the quiet confidence of a military pilot. There is something burning inside them which is that undefinable power of knowing.

Once you truly connect with your own power, it will help take your business to the next level. Your power will be increased as long as you remember that it is not just yours personally. Do not allow your power to become a conceit or a self-delusion. Connect with your power in silence, in meditation, in joy. The power is truly yours. Remember to use it properly!

Plan

What's the Plan?

As an entrepreneur you will have to create a plan for your business and for the launch of your product and services. Planning is obviously very critical for the success of your business. As you plan your moves, write them down and make your plan as clear and concise as possible so your team can understand the plan.

Have planning sessions with your team members as often as needed in order to make certain that they understand the plan and know precisely how they will implement it. You have probably heard the expression, 'Plan your work, and work your plan!' Your plan is the road map to your company's destination.

Start by planning the small steps. One step at a time is a good strategy for moving forward. When the time is right, you start to implement the bigger steps you have planned for the company. Stick with your plan unless it is absolutely necessary to change it.

When a basketball team gets on the court, the coaches have made certain that each player knows the game plan. The game plan has been diligently practiced, each player knows where they need to be on the court and what their role is in helping to win the game. If the other team creates unforeseen problems (just like it happens in business), the coaches will alter the starting game plan. Understand the intrinsic nature of plans in order to win!

Personal

Take It Personally!

Every entrepreneur must take their business personally because the business is a public demonstration of who they are, what they stand for and what they are made of from the inside out. By this I mean that you are the person in whom trust has been bestowed, so you must look at your enterprise as a personal endeavor. Doing so holds you responsible for all your undertakings, as well as those of your employees.

Being accountable to your supplier, buyer, and manufacturer is what allows you to form the necessary relationships that will enhance your business. For example, it is your personal guarantee that bills will be paid and that orders will be delivered in a timely manner that generates confidence in your creditors and customers.

My friend Eddie owned a bustling and very profitable Italian restaurant. Every night he was at the door smiling, greeting and chatting with each diner personally, offering to buy them a drink if the wait was a little long. All the while, Eddie was spreading personal goodwill which has a genuine financial value. People loved coming to Eddie's and they loved telling their friends about what a great personal experience they always had at his restaurant.

Taking personal responsibility goes a long way in the business world, so hold yourself accountable for your promises and commitments, as well as for all the wonderful personal relationships you make along the way to success.

Pace

Proper Pacing

Entrepreneurs must understand the pace of their business, the pace of their suppliers, the pace of their team and their clients' pace. Understanding pace is especially important as expenditures are going out and you are waiting for payables to come in. Therefore, you must pace all the important moving parts of your business, making adjustments in agile and skillful ways, just as an orchestral conductor paces all of the different sections of their orchestra in order to make grand music together.

Filling manufacturing orders must be done at a pace that allows for timely delivery. You want to stay ahead of the curve by keeping pace of your business' momentum, where energy is surging and where it is lapsing. Pace your purchases in order to get the best deals. And don't forget to pace yourself, keeping your physical, mental and spiritual health. Bad pace makes waste!

Master entrepreneurs see the long and wide perspectives in front of them and know how to time their moves. You are in this for the long haul, so get to understand the pace for you and your organization. Develop the skills and insight needed in order to create the best pace on the wonderful journey to success.

Q

Quota

Understand Quotas!

One way an entrepreneur conducts a review of how effectively their business is doing is by establishing quotas and reviewing the results of the company's effectiveness in reaching their quotas. A quota can be defined as the basic minimum of particular activity that needs to be reached for minimum success.

Setting your quotas will clarify the goals for what needs to be accomplished by your team each calendar quarter. Conducting a quarterly review of your sales and overall business quotas helps you to properly gage the overall performance of your business, as well as the future needs of your enterprise.

Set clearly defined quotas for sales, marketing, advertising, product launch, customer service, and even community outreach. Quotas are set by your leadership and attainment of those quotas can be motivated by setting performance bonuses. Reaching your sales goals is a sign that your team is performing at its best, your leadership is of a high quality and your future growth is predictable as it expands. Fulfill your quotas and then see about exceeding your quotas!

Quantity

Ascertaining Quantity

Entrepreneurs seeking to launch a product are mindful of the quantity of units that need to manufactured, as well as the varying costs in producing more or less inventory. The more product that is manufacturered, the lower the costs. However, a word of caution, you only want to produce the amount you can sell.

You don't want a lot of your money sitting in your warehouse in the form of unsold quantities of inventory. Understand the concept of just-in-time-inventory; that is, having enough inventory to fill orders in time but not too much inventory sitting around not earning income. Therefore, I recommend that you take preorders so you will have an idea of what is the right quantity for a particular product's projected sales.

You certainly want to avoid 'Clearance Sales.' Understanding quantity is both an art and a science. You are trying to limit speculation and, at the same time, make a reasonable projection when ordering your products. Understand this important business principle of quantity and you will avoid over-spending in one area or being stretched out if you need to plow money into another area. Of course, quality is of paramount importance but understanding quantity is oftentimes just as important as quality.

Qualifications

How Important Are They?

Before you take the leap into becoming an entrepreneur, you may hear a lot of questions about qualifications. Life's experiences are what qualified me, not a degree or a certification. One can be a successful autodidact; that is, someone who is self-taught.

Granted, some businesses require qualifying licensing based on educational requirements such being a licensed in-home health care worker or licensed general contractor. Other businesses require expertise that can only come from being qualified in specialized areas such as the medical professions, accounting, plumbing, etc. Earning a business degree such as an MBA can teach you a lot about business that will help you avoid unnecessary trial and error experiences, saving you time and money and accelerating your ultimate success.

Nevertheless, a formal education is not absolutely necessary for many businesses if you, the entrepreneur, are willing to learn hands-on how to operate your business successfully. Even if you have a special education in your business field, the main qualification still will be a desire and enough heart to believe in yourself and achieving your goals.

I know of entrepreneurs who never went to school, and some who dropped out in the third grade who became very successful. I, myself, dropped out in the ninth grade, and I have made millions of dollars, so don't let a lack of educational qualifications rob you of your destiny. Your gifts and talents were given to you by your Creator in order for you to bless humanity, not just to achieve wealth.

Be willing to trust in your natural ability and your objectives even if others don't believe in your qualifications. Pure intentions and right efforts will see you through. These are the primary qualifications for an entrepreneur.

Quick

Take Action!

As an entrepreneur, I personally believe in doing things quickly. If you have an idea and are serious about being a beneficial presence on the planet plus having an exciting and successful business life, get to work as fast as possible on developing the necessary components of your enterprise. I firmly believe that if you study too long, you're going to study wrong. By doing that, you may contradict your gut feelings, or allow destructive fear to take over your entrepreneurial vision.

Also, too much waiting can create doubts in your mind about the value of your ideas, or that your competition is too strong, or uncertainty about whether you actually have the qualifications or abilities to follow your business dream. Be quick to do your research and study, gather up funds and find your dream team, then go for your launch.

Get to work! The fruits of your labor will pay off. The quicker you activate your business, the more momentum you will gather toward your goals. Procrastination and self-imposed blockages are definite dream killers. Most people never take action, even when they come up with million dollar ideas.

Being hasty sometimes is good. Be quick or you may quit before you start.

Quality

Don't Overlook It!

Your product or service needs to be of uncompromising quality. Your entrepreneurial success is dependent on your clients loving your offering, buying it again and telling others about its amazing quality. The reason that I say this is because the average consumer prefers quality over quantity. A satisfied customer will give you unsolicited and unpaid advertising dollar value.

I have known several entrepreneurs who sold shoddy products, made quick fortunes, and then had to close up shop. The high quality of your offering will not only keep you sustained in your business but will take you beyond your expected success. You do not want your product ending up unsold or clients discontinuing your service because of quality issues.

Most people are even willing to pay extra for a quality product or service. Your quality offering will outsell the competitors. Don't you want to be recognized for the quality of your product or service? Be mindful that you intend to be an entrepreneur for a long time. Quality always wins over in time.

R

Rent

Pros and Cons

An entrepreneur must think about their physical workspace, whether you are selling a product or a service. The question comes down to: rent, lease or own? The worst part of paying rent is that it has the tendency to always go up. Of course, you can find cheaper rents in less desirable industrial or undeveloped areas.

I have only had one experience with rent coming down due to certain negligence by the owner in not properly maintaining their property. Several times when renting booths and kiosks for daily rates at street fairs and concerts, I have had to deal with greedy promoters who didn't care if I made a profit or not. All they wanted was their very high rent.

Before renting, unless you find the exact location you want and are ready to pay premium rates, please keep hunting for your perfect business location and use your third eye. Remember your intentions and mission, and the Universe will open up a better opportunity for you.

The benefit in renting, even month to month, is that you can fold up and leave a lot easier than you can terminate a lease contract. If you have to terminate a lease early, you will find that some owners will attempt to collect all the lease payments due for the entire duration of the lease, whether the place is empty for a few months or quickly leased out by them.

Therefore, be mindful when renting, leasing or purchasing property. These decisions require careful analysis and foresight by the entrepreneur.

Resolution

Be a Business Sage

As an entrepreneur, you must know how to bring conflicts, disagreements or miscommunications to a fair and equitable resolution. Finding resolution requires a maturity of judgement. Seeking the proper resolution for manufacturer defects in your products or for unsatisfactory services must be done in a way that ultimately creates harmony and continuity, creating a win-win situation for all.

Having access to mediation services in order to resolve disputes can save you a lot of time, money and most importantly, avoid losing goodwill. Entrepreneurs must know when and how to constructively resolve complaints or disagreements, in the office or outside the office. Wise and timely resolutions to challenges allow you more time and energy to focus on your business.

You always want to avoid the expenses and headaches of litigation. Make every effort to save yourself and your business from unresolved or poorly resolved setbacks. Resolution of grievances involves compromise and some letting go by both parties. You should be the one to exercise leadership and wisdom during one of those unpleasant and unavoidable business moments by demonstrating the sagacity of just resolution.

Retirement

Entrepreneurs and Retirement

Even the most successful entrepreneurs will contemplate retirement at some point. You need a retirement plan. Take into account the following things: the age that you want to retire and an exit strategy for the sale or continuation of your business. Too many entrepreneurs are fully in the dynamics of their business and don't really think about their own personal future.

But there may come a time when any entrepreneur may just no longer desire to work or may lose the ability to work. Create a retirement fund as early as possible because the faster that retirement fund builds equity, the more choices you have when it comes to retirement.

To help you plan where your asset allocations of that retirement fund are placed, I recommend that you hire a wealth coach, not just a financial consultant. Creating a wealth accumulation plan will assure that you maintain an acceptable lifestyle in retirement providing for all your needs. Next, you want to choose your successor, someone who is aligned with your original mission, excels in your industry sector, is passionate about the business you created and can take the business to unprecedented levels.

Entrepreneurs may have a family member or an offspring already operating in the business. However, you can't be sentimental in executing your retirement plan, so again, use your third eye to really make sound judgements regarding what happens after you exit the business. Retirement means peace of mind so carefully study all the components that will give you that happy state that every successful entrepreneur deserves. Your labor of love deserves the fruits of a happy retirement.

S

Share

Share to Show You Care!

Share the knowledge you have gained in business with your community. Many entrepreneurs miss the great opportunity to share their experience and resources with people in the community who also are seeking to make a positive impact on society. One of the ways I share is by being an active mentor in the Network for Teaching Entrepreneurship (NFTE) which is an international non-profit organization providing entrepreneurship training and education programs to young people from low-income urban communities.

Sharing is a way of caring. The good of sharing always comes back to you and your business. Note that today there is a huge 'sharing economy' such as peer-to-peer lending, crowdfunding, apartment/house renting and couch surfing, ridesharing and car sharing, co-working. Note also that open-source companies such as Google who give away free email and web searching, or Facebook whose 2.5 billion users on earth use their service for free, are some of the biggest and richest companies on earth.

Therefore, look at your business to see what you can share. What can your company afford to share with your clients and your community? Time, education, closeout or clearance items? Remember that the universe is endlessly abundant and that there are unlimited resources for your business. Share and show you care, and you will be blessed beyond measure.

Speak

Be a Speaker!

Lend your voice to whatever you do, whether it is developing your product or delivering your service. Becoming a speaker is a way to gain new customers and new, innovative employees who want to be part of the vision you are articulating. Of course, many people fear public speaking. If that's you, I recommend that you start getting over your fears ASAP.

To help you get started, join a Toastmasters chapter. You'll find them all over the world. Toastmasters will help you develop your speaking and listening skills. If you are the CEO or the president or a manager, you deal with the public and possibly the news media.

Starting to hone your public speaking skills now will fast track you into doing business in a more professional manner. You'll find that you don't stumble over your words as much, you are communicating better and that you are learning the very valuable skill of listening to others as well. People trust and follow a quality speaker in business, politics, religious affairs and science.

Develop your 'elevator pitch,' that ten second spoken delivery of what your company does. Speaking clearly, enunciating and using correct grammar are skills that will definitely help you to develop meaningful relationships with the public and with your employees and associates, all of which are factors in your expanding business empire.

Schedule

Your Schedule is Your Friend!

As an entrepreneur, you must know how to keep yourself on a tight schedule. Scheduling allows you to maximize your energy and efforts in real time. Scheduling allows you to organize your day in the most productive manner and helps you to eliminate counterproductive activities.

Beware of the Time Bandits! They will try to steal your time and get you off your schedule. Your schedule provides you the means to more readily make necessary changes and modifications even with the inevitable disruptions that will occur in your business day.

Write your schedule down at night so that the next day you have created a time line that includes all of the things that you need to do that day. Your schedule includes time for morning meditation and prayer, showering, dressing, eating, work meetings and phone calls, emails, research, attending meetings, exercise, socializing, volunteering, and relaxing.

Your schedule allows you to create priorities. Be careful not to get over-ambitious with your schedule. Avoid stressing yourself out. The schedule is meant to keep you on track to achieve your goals.

Score

A Great Score!

As a longtime and successful entrepreneur, I want to share with you a valuable tip on how to educate yourself through different channels as you navigate through your entrepreneurial efforts. SCORE organization has been extremely helpful to me over the years. At SCORE you will meet experienced business mentors and get a variety of educational business insights.

SCORE is made up of retired and active businessmen and businesswomen volunteers who have gone through many more phases of business activities than you as a beginning entrepreneur. The volunteers know what to give back to their community of up and coming entrepreneurs through one-on-one mentoring. Your local Small Business Association (SBA) will connect you with a SCORE representative.

Once you are assigned to a counselor, be open, friendly and available to the wisdom that he or she has to offer you. As you gain the necessary insights into being a successful entrepreneur, you are using a special leverage of knowledge gained from experienced sources. You do not want to reinvent the wheel, so ask questions and solicit the best advice you can get through this wonderful organization. This learning process will enable you to eventually score big!

Sales

Know How to Ask!

Obviously as an entrepreneur, you can't undervalue the importance of sales. All businesses buy and sell. People who work only for a salary (and this is not a put-down) don't experience the thrills and chills of sales. However, I have seen entrepreneurs who seem to be afraid of selling. By that I mean that I have seen creative and earnest young entrepreneurs become timid when asking potential customers for their business.

Sales are all about asking. Of course, there are many ways of asking for people's business. That is an entire book in and of itself. Fear of rejection is what can keep an entrepreneur from asking for and getting a sale. And that fear may not even manifest itself in an obvious manner. There are numerous ways all of us can manage to self-sabotage.

Sales is both an art and a science, never easy. You've heard the expression, "He's a born salesman." Not all entrepreneurs are "born salesmen" but great sales techniques can be learned. The more you study the masters and learn their successful sales techniques, the more confident and eager you will become in going out to get your sales. You already know you have a terrific product or service to offer. Now you need to know how to get the customer to give that final Yes! and sign the deal.

Learn and practice the art of asking. A Bible scripture cautions that "You do not have because you do not ask." Actually, the whole scripture (in James 4:2-3) reads "You do not have because you do not ask God." Of course, as a spiritual entrepreneur, you have to understand and start with that premise. The sooner you learn to ask of both God and man, the faster and more lucrative your business will grow.

You should know that people actually like or even love being asked for their business, especially if you have a product or service that they need or can use. Sales can be exhilarating! Sometimes sales are a roller coaster ride but loving to sell has to be part of your entrepreneurial spirit.

Save

You Can Save!

Entrepreneurs sometimes have a hard time thinking about saving. Usually, you will be the last person in your enterprise to be paid, especially in any new venture. The money that the business earns has to be used to pay employees, pay for manufacturing, rent and electricity, repayment of loans, investor percentages and a host of other payables that sometimes are not matched by receivables.

If this is your early experience, don't get frustrated. As a small tangible sign of the return for your time, money and energy contributions to the business, allow yourself even a small token of payment, even if is only $100 a week. This small contribution to yourself can also be seen as part of your savings plan. If your business soars from Day One, great! Figure out what you can take home and of that amount set aside a percentage for your savings account, even if it is only 10% of your take home.

Working and working, and in the end not having much to show for our labors is counterproductive. Start to save right from the start of your venture. As your savings increase, of course you start to feel more relaxed about the future. And don't forget to tithe to a charity or your place of worship. There is a very strong and positive energy in saving!

T

Task

Know Your Task!

An entrepreneur does not fear the word task. A task is defined simply as a piece of work to be done or undertaken. As an entrepreneur you have one main task: to be willing to take the risk to gain a substantial outcome. Yes, this is a big task!

Ask yourself if you are really ready to expend your heart and soul, your financial resources as well as hitting up your family and friends for favors, and in general really going out on a limb. Taking on the task of building your entrepreneurial empire is no small undertaking. Make sure you are ready for this amazing task spiritually, physically, emotionally and mentally.

Once you are committed to taking on this herculean task, you can start to task others. You must learn to delegate specific tasks to your team. In turn, each team member must be instructed as to how to allocate the necessary resources to complete their task. Each task should have a specific order of operation, date of completion, and a pre-determined and completely understood outcome that you, the taskmaster, will be pleased to accept. Knowing who to assign to what specific tasks, when those assignments should be made and how these assigned tasks fit into your strategic goals must be executed with skill and insight by you. Understand the task at hand!

Tactics

Understand Tactics!

Entrepreneurs are always thinking about decisions and moves that they need to make from both a tactical and strategic point of view. Remember, tactics refer to the skill of dealing with or handling immediate situations, to achieve a specific goal. Strategy is defined as a comprehensive high-level, long-term plan. Being tactical focuses on specific tasks, concrete smaller steps, best practices, specific procedures, and resources. Strategy is the overall campaign plan, which may involve complex operational patterns, activity, and decision-making that govern tactical execution.

To be a successful entrepreneur, you must understand and learn to execute both tactics and strategy. Like a game of chess, business is a measured activity in which you want to make decisions that will benefit the bottom line and ensure that your customers keep doing business with you. With that in mind, devise tactics and strategies that will enable you to reach your goals in a rational, thought-out manner.

Setting up and maintaining reliable statistical analyses of your business activities is a smart tactic that allows you to quantify the value of your decisions by revealing which ones have or have not been beneficial. Also, keeping a running tab on your key indicators allows you to change tactics within your strategic plan. Stay on top of your tactics!

Taxes

Knowing Taxes!

Entrepreneurs know that they must research the ways and means to lower their tax liabilities. If you don't know enough about the current tax laws, get advice from your accountant or do the internet research. Tax planning is part of both your tactical and strategic approach to maximizing profits legally.

To defer your research into your business's tax advantages and liabilities can cause you interest and penalties. Familiarize yourself with any tax breaks that may apply to your business so you can retain as much of your capital as possible. Taxes are crucial to the overall well-being of our cities, states, and the country as a whole. However, as an entrepreneur, your job is to reduce your tax burden while always being a good, tax-paying citizen.

Tax research has helped me to find tax incentives. For example, The Disabled Access Credit is a refundable annual tax credit for making a business accessible to persons with disabilities that is available to small businesses, according to the Internal Revenue Code, Section 44. The Work Opportunity Tax Credit (WOTC) is a federal tax credit available to employers who hire and retain individuals from target groups with significant employment barriers (e.g., veterans, ex-felons, etc.). Employers can claim about $9,600 per employee in tax credits per year under the WOTC program.

A smart entrepreneur can take advantage of opportunities like these to save your capital for other business-related expenses such as sales and marketing. Understanding taxes does not have to be taxing!

Team

T.E.A.M.

Entrepreneurs understand the necessity of putting together the right team for their enterprise. The acronym, TEAM stands for 'Together Everybody Achieves More.' This has been my mantra in situations where I am organizing my team to reach sales goals or strategizing to bring my product or service to the market.

Knowing how to work together with different types of people is essential for entrepreneurs. And as they say in professional sports, there is no letter I in the word team. Every individual on your team has a contribution that is important but you do have to be careful with the stars on your team not becoming too conceited or departing from the team plan. Achieving company goals is never the responsibility of a lone player but the outcome of a multitude of key players working together. Every team member works to bring about a common goal.

Once you realize the importance of forming a team of individuals who can work together and who know exactly what their assignments are, the faster you will reach your goal. Team building is a key attribute for a successful entrepreneurship, involves finding the right players who can come together to get the job done. Remember T.E.A.M.

Technology

You Can't Live Without It!

Entrepreneurs today must know how to use technology tools. When I first started out as an entrepreneur in the late 60's, I had no knowledge of what technology could do for me. Fast forward to the mid-80's when technology became a household item. I had to learn to use the available technology or be left behind by my competitors.

Using technology allows entrepreneurs to peek into every aspect of their industry group and not just keep up, but also gain the momentum to leap in front of the competition. You must connect to technology through the internet and specific apps for (1) research, (2) tutorials from sales and marketing gurus, (3) learning new technologies that the smart entrepreneur can graft onto their own service or product, (4) to start blogging and vlogging, (5) and to learn how to monetize your YouTube channel.

Make technology your silent partner and you will certainly find ways to gain on the competition and sprint past them too.

Think

Understand Thinking!

Entrepreneurs, let's start with the obvious on this topic: What is thinking? To think means the mental process in which one direct one's mind toward someone or something; uses one's mind actively to form connected ideas or manipulate information, as when we form concepts, engage in problem solving, use reason and make decisions. The act of thinking produces thoughts.

As an entrepreneur, think through situations and circumstances. Dr. Pat Allen, world-renowned psychotherapist says, "Feel, think, act." Too often we feel, then act. This advice may seem obvious but it really is something that a lot of passionate entrepreneurs fail to do. Take the time to think about what the overall best outcome will be for your business product launch or service.

As you consider your opportunity to make a difference for humanity, think through what your decisions will look like, and then determine how to move forward. Understanding consequences, or in spiritual terms karma, is a sign of personal and business maturity.

The classic American self-help book As You Think by James Allen reminds us that "All we achieve and all that we fail to achieve is the direct result of our own thoughts." It is imperative for us to train our minds to think on the highest good and how we can manifest that good for ourselves, our families and friends, our employees, and our collective community.

Therefore, be constant and vigilant in training your mind to think in a constructive manner, and you will bring forth something positive, personally and businesswise.

Thrifty

Being Thrifty is Good!

I started all of my first businesses on a shoe string budget. I had to learn the meaning of the word thrifty from the get-go. You probably are not aware but the etymology of the word thrifty is from the Middle English denoting a sense of prosperity, acquired wealth, success; and from Old Norse, from thrífa meaning to grasp or get hold of something.

Today, the usage of the adjective thrifty implies a person or their behavior in using money and other resources carefully and not wastefully. If you want your business to prosper, exercise caution in using both your personal money and the money you receive from investors. This is how being thrifty creates prosperity.

In addition, be thrifty with all of the resources that you use to grow and develop your enterprise. The reason to use your resources carefully and wisely is that the opposite of that is to create a waste of your money, time, and resources.

Not understanding thriftiness will doom your business so keep the word thrifty in your consciousness. Before you act, think it through: Is this really the thrifty way to proceed? Develop the habits of thrift and you will see the benefits to your business accumulate rapidly.

Track

Tracking Your Customers!

Obviously, today we see the importance in every aspect of tracking from weather to cargo to facial recognition in police work. Entrepreneurs can now track just about everything necessary for the viability of their businesses. Tracking is essential for any modern thriving business.

With the technological tracking devises that we have today, we can track our client database, shipments, sales, and inventory. It is possible with customized computer software to track the number of items sold, as well as when and where they were sold.

We entrepreneurs can use customer service surveys to assist us in tracking what causes our customers to do business with us and what we can do to better serve them. Shoppers today have become very sophisticated and they do a lot of their research online.

Maybe you were doing a search for a flight to Shanghai. All of a sudden, you see pop-up ads you from Cheapo Air on Shanghai flights. How did they find out you were interested in a flight to Shanghai? How is it that their flights to Shanghai are now popping up on your screen without permission?

Tracking personal choices and trends empowers businesses today to individually tailor their marketing materials to anyone that comes near their researched product or service sector. Learn what it really means to track the details of your customers' preferences and then learn how to utilize that information to offer your customers the best product or service opportunities you have to give them.

Trade

Being a Real Trader!

In past centuries, being in a trade meant that you were in some guild such as ironsmiths, cobblers, livery, tailors, etc. Nowadays, you are entered into a particular trade called an industry sector. Know your trade! Know the other members of your trade. Become a member in your trade associations to learn more and do better deals. Know the trends within your trade and also those of affiliated trades.

Remember also that a trader is literally one who barters. Barter is the original form of business and has existed since man first appeared on the planet. Today, barter trade is a multi-billion dollar aspect of business that even the IRS recognizes and taxes. American Airlines needs rooms from Hilton hotels for its pilots and flight attendants. Hilton hotels needs airline travel for its executives. Hilton and American Airlines figure out the value of rooms and flights and then they trade rooms for flights, and flights for rooms. Of course, there is a monetary value assessed on these trades but money never exchanges hands.

If you, as a trader, can truly study the art and science of barter, you will save lots of money, sell unused inventory and you will find numerous new opportunities. Check out ITEX, the largest barter exchange in the world. Become a member. Once you understand this kind of trading, whole new opportunities will open up for you, especially in times when business slows down. Using trade in its most basic forms will give you advantages that your competitors may have missed. Understand trade in all its many aspects!

Trust

Trust in What?

If you think about it, everything we do is based on trust. When you turn on the tap water, you trust that the water will not have tasteless and lethal cyanide that is oftentimes found in rural water wells. When you drive in traffic, you trust the signal lights.

Everywhere you look, trust is in play. Children trust parents. Parents trust the schools. You can think of innumerable examples right in your own life of trust. Every entrepreneur must learn the importance of trust in business. To trust someone, they must first earn your trust, same as you earning their trust.

You trust that your suppliers or your employees will deliver what they state they will deliver. Your clients trust the claims you make on your product or service. You must build that trust. Reliability and durability are factors that you advertise about your product or service.

You have seen signs like: In business since 1992! Of course, that is meant to instill trust in the proprietor's offering to the public. Your team members need to trust you, as you need to trust them. Are you keeping your commitments? Are they keeping their commitments?

Trust has to build in and around your organization, and with the public. Sometimes references and testimonials are needed to build trust. Mistrust causes fear and eventually a breakdown. In spiritual terms, we read in Psalms 18:30: "God is a shield to all those who trust Him." The trust you build with your team, your clients and your community is not only your protection but it is ultimately the only way to move forward to entrepreneurial success!

u

Unite

Unite To Help Others

Entrepreneurs unite! As an entrepreneur who has been doing business for over fifty years, and has made millions of dollars, I suggest that you find it in your heart to help aspiring entrepreneurs so they can meet you and learn from your expertise.

I prefer speaking in a classroom and also volunteering. Unite with organizations that will appreciate your informed presentation where you share your knowledge with the next generation of entrepreneurs. As previously mentioned, the National Foundation for Teaching Entrepreneurship (NFTE) is one such organization that teaches kids ages 11 to 18 how to create business and marketing plans, and other important business concepts.

You can also unite with and share your entrepreneurial experiences with Operation Hope who state their mission as "Working to disrupt poverty and empower low income youth and adults to equip them with the financial tools and education to facilitate the journey to financial independence."

You can unite with Junior Achievement, whose programs "Help prepare young people for the real world by showing them how to generate wealth and effectively manage it, how to create jobs which make their communities more robust." I have united with all these organization who are driven by volunteer businesspeople.

I know that you too will be providing a great service if you take the time to unite with these types of organizations and share the truths you have gained about business, as well as your personal triumphs and failures. Let's unite with our next generation of business leaders and demonstrate our sincere interest in the promising possibilities for their future.

Universal

Learn Universal Laws!

At this point in reading my book, you probably understand the imperative that every truly successful entrepreneur must build their business on a spiritual foundation of universal principles. For some entrepreneurs it take a long time to come to this important understanding. These universal principles are not secret but unfortunately there are those well-meaning entrepreneurs who think there are only some highly paid experts who will reveal these hidden, classified truths.

Let me be that expert for you, here and now, and reveal to you just one beautiful universal law; namely, that we all live in a friendly Universe. Believe it or not, the Universe is really on your side. God loves you and needs you.

If your desire is to create business products and services is not just based on financial motives but primarily for the well-being of humanity and nature, you can bet that the Universe will support you by opening up doors to opportunities beyond your wildest imagination. People and money will show up in your life to help you work to realize the purest intentions you have set for your endeavors.

Things come together seemingly out of nowhere but in reality, the Universal Law of Divine Energy is always seeking a bigger and greater expression of itself for the greater good of humankind. Furthermore, know that universal laws remain constant, allowing you to predict not exactly how your entrepreneurial vision will manifest but allowing you to keep steadfast in your heart and mind that all the good in that vision is truly magnificent and imminent.

Study universal principles and laws, being ever mindful of them as you go forth to multiply the consciousness of the All-Good. Always remember that you are universally supported from the moment you had the inspiration for your business to the realization of your eventual business success.

Union

The Value of Union

As an entrepreneur, you have the ability to bring people together for a common interest, purpose or good through union. The opposite of union is disunion, or chaos. Union creates harmonious agreements, not only for the sole purpose of bringing forth a successful product or service.

When you can facilitate a union among your people, your chance of becoming successful accelerates, and also a sense of belonging and worth is created among your team. Study after study has shown that people really appreciate their job much more for the respect and value that an employer shows them rather than for their compensation. How is this job appreciation accomplished?

If you study any great leader--corporate, government, military or religious—or, if you have had the opportunity to work with a great leader, you understand that these great leaders possess the single, impressive ability to bring people together for the common good. Effective leaders understand the value of unifying people. Worker's unions are also based on gathering together for the greater good.

Any unified organization always works better than a fragmented one, wherein individual motives dominate. The expression, "The whole is greater than the sum of its parts" was first coined by the philosopher Aristotle, and aptly defines the modern concept of synergy. In union, we operate with greater precision. You have also heard the expression, "United we stand, divided we fall."

The spiritual Sanskrit Indian word yoga means union, and the process by which we can achieve the union of body, mind and spirit. Consider the common good for your company by always working toward the cohesiveness known as union.

Uniform

Uniforms Help Your Business!

Entrepreneurs work every angle that will give their business an advantage. I have been asked by several business owners if their employees should wear a uniform. My reply is always, "Yes!"

There is a subtle yet powerful spirit in the word uniform. The prefix uni means one, and form derives from the Latin for a likeness or image. A uniform signifies an image of oneness in your team which creates togetherness for the entire company good.

Uniforms play an important role in any organization. They act as an identification mark for customers to spot your company employees. Employees also get rid of spending their time and money for special office or business clothes. Uniforms help to market, advertise and create awareness of your company's brand. Another advantage of a company uniform is that the uniform provides a professional image to clients, giving them a greater sense of confidence and trust in the company. Uniforms provide safety, protection and security to employees.

And again, uniforms promote team building. Understand the benefits of a company uniform and you will certainly see positive results.

Unequivocal

Can You Be Unequivocal?

As an entrepreneur, I am unequivocal about the information I am providing to you in this book. This information will unequivocally transform your life and business. I am not being conceited here. I am simply making an unequivocal statement. Stating things in unequivocal terms signifies your confidence and expertise.

The principles and techniques I am describing to you have been used by sage business owners for thousands of years. I have used them myself to generate millions of dollars over my more than half a century of business dealings. Study (and restudy) these important principles and techniques, then implement them in order to experience the unequivocal effectiveness of what is being taught here.

Begin with the unequivocal fact that your true purpose on our earth journey is to embody the joy, love and light. This simple fact has to be imprinted in your consciousness from the minute you wake up till you get back to your restful sleep. All of humanity can embrace this simple unequivocal fact, irrespective of ethnicity, culture or religious preference.

Think about it: Where do you want you go every day but further up in your personal and business endeavors? That has to be an unequivocal, foundational truth for you. Unequivocal derives from the Latin word equivocaes meaning a word or expression capable of different and equal voice (or meaning). Therefore unequivocal denotes of unequal voice — meaning, unmistakable, unambiguous, unique or without question.

Are you ready, as an entrepreneur, to be one of an unequivocal voice, whose expression and output is real, unmistakable and unique?

Ultimate

Always Bring Your Ultimate

As an entrepreneur, my ultimate goal is to give you quantifiable information that will assist you in becoming the ultimate entrepreneur. To do anything to the ultimate means that you give it your all. You are offering your very best based on your greatest intentions, efforts and means.

And if you think about it, the fuel that powers the ultimate performance of artists, athletes, surgeons, astronauts, teachers, sales professionals and corporate heads is love. When you love what you do, others will feel your passion. And remember, true passion has no limits.

Before a real entrepreneur even takes the first initiating steps in their endeavor, they know intuitively that ultimately there is no end, that there are many more dimensions to explore even beyond the stated goals of their endeavors. Being the ultimate doesn't mean you are competing with others. It is simply all about you bringing your best game on the playing field, and looking for every opportunity to always better your best game.

Every successful man, woman and child, in any field, comes on the playing field with an ironclad knowing that they have the ability to express their unique, winning genius no matter how big or bad their competition looks. And giving your ultimate raises everybody's game.

When players went up against Kobe Bryant, their own game improved dramatically. The ultimate energy of Kobe Bryant was inspiring to everybody he played with or against. Giving your ultimate self in your business you will certainly positively affect your team, your clients and your community. Giving your ultimate effort is some of the best free advertising you can get.

Yes, people do feel the energy of a top performer, even when they just enter the room. Always seek to bring out that ultimate aspect of yourself, and your business and profits will ultimately even surprise you.

V

Value

Know Your Values!

As an entrepreneur, you must understand both your own value as well as what you value in your life. Oftentimes, our estimations of our values may not be accurate. You probably know some conceited persons who over-value their importance. Or you may know an individual who is too modest or is undervaluing themselves.

Getting an accurate fix on ourselves, either in the mirror or in the world, is not always easy. Should we self-validate or look for validation from others, or from our achievements? Once we realize our true God-given value, both as an individual and as part of the collective, we can move into all areas of our lives—business, social, family, communal, spiritual—with greater confidence and self-worth.

How we value our business, the value of our goods and services, of our team members must be based on accurate and rational assessments. Once you realize the true value of your business, you can begin to decide how to monetize these values.

Create a mission statement that explains the values that your product or service brings to your customers. Your honest and realistic valuation lets the public know what to expect from your offerings. People feel comfortable aligning with you when they have a clear idea of who you are, what your company stands for, and what the product or service does for them.

Of course, you will do the math before you put your product or service out in the market to properly determine how to make a profit. However, make an honest valuation of yourself, your business and its valuable place in the world of commerce before you take the first concrete steps in your enterprise. Know the value of proper valuations!

Vigilant

Entrepreneurs must be ever vigilant. To be vigilant means to keep a careful watch for danger or difficulties. While rising to the pinnacle of your business, you will encounter challenges, necessitating that you keep a careful watch on as many facets of your enterprise as humanly possible all along. Along the way, remain vigilant as signs will warn you of problems on the horizon.

How does one remain vigilant? Mindfulness. Mindfulness means that the mind is full of the awareness of reality. When we drift out of that awareness our vision becomes somewhat blurry and our hearing is somewhat reduced. If you stay vigilant, in reality as it is and not in fantasy, you increase your sharpness and intelligence.

Everyone should know the famous lyric from Kenny Roger's song The Gambler, "You got to know when to hold them, and when to fold them." Indeed, being an entrepreneur is like being a gambler. Note that I am speaking of professional gamblers who keep their cool and are always reasoning, strategizing and vigilant, not like the unfortunate loser gambling addicts. The key is being vigilant, entirely focused in reality.

As an important aside, each morning in your meditation and prayer, practice the art of vigilantly remaining breath by breath in the present moment, even noting when your mind has drifted from the moment. In pray, activate that vigilance through addressing the Creator to keep you ever-present and vigilant for the signs, wonders and miracles that abound all around us.

I say that you, as a successful entrepreneur, will be one who remains vigilant, focused and true to the core values and principles that are in your mission statement. Despite the difficulties and risks inherent in any entrepreneurial venture, when you remain vigilant of your core values and they are fundamentally in tune with the betterment of life, then all the forces of the Universe will align with you, and nothing can stop the natural flow of the highest good from accelerating for you. Keep vigilant to both your day-to-day business, as well as to your foundational values!

Versatile

The Advantages of Being Versatile!

Entrepreneurs need to always remain versatile as you move forward, pivot and move relentlessly toward your goals. Notice that basketball players from time to time dribble directly toward the basket and lay up the ball. Other times, they charge forward, back up, move left or right, pass the ball or shoot if there is a split second opportunity to do so. Versatility!

You have to be able to adapt to and respect rules in life in order to be successful, and sometimes you have to bend or break rules—as long as you stay legal and ethical. Wending your way in business requires expansion, pause, assimilation, turnarounds, all kinds of moves, planned or unplanned. You, as the team leader, will have to make marketing and advertising decisions, manufacturing and distribution choices, hiring and firing judgements, sometimes on a weekly basis.

Being versatile means to be able to adapt or change to different functions, activities and circumstances. The successful entrepreneur knows every corner of their empire which allows them to make moves based on their comprehensive understanding of all the business's assets and liabilities.

Starting small gives you the versatility of being more agile and quick than the big boys. Obviously, the bigger your business becomes, the more layered and slower decisions become in changing directions or innovating in unfamiliar areas. This corporate slowness has allowed the versatile entrepreneur to gain faster entry into newer or more lucrative areas of their sector than the bigger corporate entities. Also, during slower, leaner times, your more versatile team will be open to new and even novel ways to achieve your goals.

Versatility also means that you the boss may sometime even have to pick up a wrench and get under the sink to fix a leaky pipe. Therefore, always be willing to be versatile because versatility is your leverage for sustainability and success!

175

Venture

Venture Forth!

You, as an entrepreneur, must understand that the whole game of entrepreneurship as a venture in excitement. Remember when we were kids and our parents said we were going on an adventure? We got really excited and couldn't wait to get out of the house into our adventure.

The difference between venture and adventure is that a venture is a risky, daring undertaking or journey while an adventure is that which happens without design, by chance and implies some danger. Every venture in life is a bold, daring, and audacious move in the direction of your heart's desires. The majority of people hesitate to venture out because when embarking on an uncertain undertaking, trust and confidence must accompany us.

We entrepreneurs learn to trust in our bold venture because we know that our venture will add value to someone's life. We are not only living out our dreams but we are helping others to realize their dreams also. When we take on our venture with this kind of trust—in our mission, ourselves and our team—we discover that we are definitely supported by that higher power that gives us everything we need to flourish and shine for the greater good.

The demonstration of that support is inevitable and if you are truly mindful you will start to see subtle signs, a little wink or nod from the Universe itself, to let you know that your efforts are noted. Those signs start to build your confidence until more and more concrete aspects of your business venture start to manifest and point the way to success. Remember the old adage, "Nothing ventured, nothing gained."

Victory

Knowing Victory!

Entrepreneurs must think only in terms of victory, never defeat. Think of any great artist, athlete, scientist, or surgeon. They walk into their arena of endeavor with a certain swagger that indicates they already smell victory. Never think of wanting victory in your venture as something wrong or egotistic.

A mindset of victory is part of your tool kit in the pursuit of excellence. When this mindset is in place, ask yourself, "Now what must I actually do to be victorious as I launch my product or service and move through all the necessary steps toward the ever-expanding horizon of possibilities?"

As you have heard me say numerous times by now in this book, the whole game of entrepreneurship should first be played from a foundation of service based on doing what your God-given talents have mandated you to do and that you love to do. These motives are what will spur you on to be victorious in your endeavors, loving what you do and eventually also be loved by others for your excellent offerings. Onward to Victory!

Vigor

The Importance of Vigor!

Entrepreneurs are full of vigor. Vigor is that state when we are physically strong, hardy and maintain good health. Vigor is also effort, energy, and enthusiasm. Traveling the rigorous road of entrepreneurship requires both outer and inner vigor.

You must cultivate and maintain a healthy lifestyle as the physical demands of entrepreneurship require long hours in a dynamic environment. Get ample rest and learn healthy ways to relax too. By that I mean, get into a hot tub at the end of the day, rather than ending up at the nearest pub after work.

The amount of concentration and mental power required of you, the entrepreneur, is greater than what is required of anyone else in your business. Keep your vigor by keeping away from emotional or other mental distractions.

And for your inner spiritual vigor, every morning get in some time for meditation, affirmative prayer and visioning. Even on some day when you have a busy schedule ahead of you and you only have a few moments to attend to your inner spiritual vigor, that's OK. As my own pastor says, "BTN," or Better Than Nothing! Or, as the old Amex commercials used to say, "Don't leave home without it."

Emphasizing your vigor cannot be overemphasized. Keeping up your vigor allows you to naturally exude enthusiasm for your product or service. Being vigorous requires consistent and constant attention and effort.

The vigor practices that I have described are an important factor in helping you to keep bright, outgoing, passionate and ultimately successful. Keep up your vigor!

Vicarious

For Those Watching!

Your entrepreneurial efforts are going to be scrutinized and judged—not just by your customers, your team, your family and community, your industry partners and investors—but also by so-called "innocent bystanders."

One has a vicarious experience through one's own imagination via the feelings or actions of another person. If your sister returns from her vacation in Spain and vividly recounts her travel experiences, you feel as if you have had almost the same experience just from her account, achieving a vicarious experience.

So, yes, those who are with you on the momentous journey of your entrepreneurial efforts, your struggles, the pain and joy will also be experiencing almost your same experience but from different vantage points. Now, you are not going to be intimidated or moved by those around you who are having their various vicarious experiences but if they are going to be watching the show from their particular seat, maybe you want to put on a worthwhile show. Maybe it's your son or daughter who is watching all your moves and experiencing your journey from the sidelines. Do you want them to be inspired and one day themselves experience the success of a great entrepreneurial venture?

What about the doubters, or those handicapped by the fear to strike out on their own, as you have done? You are actually creating your success story for them also. No, you are not Jesus Christ who is going to die for their sins. However, you are aware that in a certain sense your venture is going to be a teaching experience for all those who are watching you.

You are not necessarily creating your business empire to impress them or make them feel inferior but you are saying, without ego or conceit, 'See, this is what it takes to be imaginative, confident and even heroic if you want to exercise your innate greatness." Bravely living out your imagination is what being an entrepreneur is all about, so be willing to live it in a grand fashion so that others will also be inspired, even vicariously.

179

Virtue

Be Guided by Virtue!

Entrepreneurs cultivate their essential virtues before they set out on the road to success. The word virtue comes from the Latin root vir, for man. At first virtue meant manliness or valor but over time it settled into the sense of moral excellence. Virtue can also mean excellence in general. Morals are concerned with the principles of right and wrong behavior, and the goodness or badness of human character, and holding or manifesting the highest principles for proper conduct.

Sometimes we entrepreneurs want to jump start our businesses, and in our excitement we may forget about establishing the virtues of a sound and stable life structure. Remember to start with your enterprise through that mission plan which outlines the purpose and virtues of your enterprise.

Virtue is characterized by behavior that demonstrates our commitment to the best of society's values. Our virtues are on display for everyone to notice, especially consumers who are more apt to do business with someone with a high degree of morality.

If you possess and exhibit strong virtues, you will be able to remain steadfast and focused on your dreams and aspirations, especially when the storms of life come knocking at your door. Your virtues will be the guiding force that allow you to remain resolute and centered. Examine and articulate your virtues on a daily basis in order to remain mindful of your entrepreneurial purpose.

Vital

Gotta Have It!

Are you certain that your product or service is vital to your customers? Entrepreneurs understand that their offering to the public must be perceived as vital, meaning absolutely necessary, important and essential for their well-being and needs. When something is vital, it is relevant, timely, useful, and may even be considered indispensable.

What you want more than anything else is for the people you serve to consider what you are offering to be significant and important to them. You should have the perspective that each product or service that you bring into the marketplace serves a vital need, now and in the future.

I have a friend who is a multi-millionaire because he created a vital product for dog owners: creative and colorful plastic dog bowls. You see, your product or service does not need to be vital to everyone but know your target client base and offer them vital merchandise or help that they cannot pass up.

How you create that vital widget or service is the fun and creative part of your business. How you spin out and market the vital need that your customers must perceive when they see or hear about your genius innovation is also part of the inspiration and imagination that you and your team will come up with for the public. Make it vital!

Vocation

It's Not Just a Job!

Of course, entrepreneurs think that their brilliant ideas and their innovative business efforts and skills are anything but a vocation. Vocation implies graduating from a skills program such as an electrician, plumber, nurse, software programmer or some sort of job-oriented or work destination related to a common sort of profession.

However, a vocation is really defined as a strong feeling of suitability for a particular career or occupation, that is regarded as particularly worthy and requiring great dedication. So, a vocation should not be viewed as a humdrum sort of thing. One can choose to be a poet as one's vocation, or a drummer, or a deep sea diver.

Learn from the start, your chosen vocation is being an entrepreneur. You chose your exciting vocation because you have a strong feeling of suitability for it. It is truly your life's work, chosen because you love of it.

Your entrepreneurial vocation must elicit intense feelings of dedication and energy from within that will sustain you and your business for the long haul. Your vocation embodies the driving force within you that helps you accomplish your goals in offering your product or service to the public.

Along the way, you may meet some young, would-be entrepreneurs— for example, at the high schools where I mentor enthusiastic and idealist young women and men—and you will inspire them with a vocation they never thought possible.

As you experience awe and gratitude for being able to give of your gifts and live your dream, you will know that you are not simply working in a vocation. Because you are so in love with what you are doing, you might feel that you could even do your entrepreneurial song and dance simply for the love and joy that it brings you. This is the heart of true vocational work, and the best way to ultimately shape your business into a great success story.

W

World

We are the World!

For an entrepreneur, the world is their oyster. This is a quote from Shakespeare which means that you can achieve anything you wish in life or go anywhere because you have the opportunity or ability to do so. This saying is often applied to young people about to embark into adult life. It implies that everything is open to an individual, and that if one is open to the world, they can encounter something special. The metaphor that informs the saying is that if you have seen the world as your oyster, it signifies that there may be a pearl in it for you.

Today humanity is connected in ways that are unprecedented. For us entrepreneurs, it means that we can do business all over the world without even leaving the comfort of home. Thinking on a world scale is paramount for the truly creative entrepreneur. By simply clicking on a link on your computer screen, you can locate any resource, person, company, product or service in the world in an instant.

If you speak English, you can communicate with almost anyone in the business sector of the 195 countries around the world. US exports and imports of goods and services related to GDP (Gross Domestic Product) ratio is about 28% yearly. What would that mean to increase your business bottom line by 28% yearly? And of course, there are numerous US companies whose world business revenues are much higher. Caterpillar, the US manufacturer of heavy machinery, derives 58% of their revenues from foreign sales. And of course, there are numerous US small companies that also do the majority of their sales around the world.

In spite of the many differences we have in our worldviews, a common thread weaves us all together in such a way that we can exchange products and services that benefit one another. Therefore, think in terms of the whole world as your oyster, and prepare to share your gifts with the world.

Word

What Does Your Word Mean?

An entrepreneur's word is a very potent force. Be mindful of the power of the spoken word whenever you open your mouth to communicate with a team member, a supplier or your customers. In business, and of course personally, your word must be a force that manifests the highest good in the world.

If you look at any object in front of you at this moment; for example, the pen on your desk, you must understand that pen started as an idea and then through the agency of words, spoken or written, it manifested as a reality. In Genesis we read, "In the beginning was the word." Your word, spoken or unspoken, has the power to bring forth things into existence. Therefore, always be careful of what you are thinking also because that is what you are wishing on a person or on your own reality.

Your word gives people a glimpse into what you truly possess, as well as what you are trying to possess or accomplish. Your actions are judged by the words that predate them. You said you would deliver the product order on Friday, didn't you? You gave your word and if the action does not suit the word, what are the consequences to your business? Your word must always be in alignment with your actions. If you can't deliver on time, call the client with advance notice and simply say, "I'm very sorry. I promised we could deliver on Friday but now this has happened and there will be a delay."

When your words and actions are the same, you are properly aligned with reality. You have heard the expression, "My word is my bond." Yes, in the business world, deals large and small have been consummated by two parties who have trust in the verbal contract they made together. And by the way, a verbal contract is the same as a written contract by law.

With your words, be articulate, accurate, concise and clear. You will see all the good-will assets that accrue from this oftentimes overlooked important factor, especially at the beginning of your entrepreneurial efforts. Stay true to your word and the Universe will make the truth of your word become more and more of a reality each time you speak or write your word.

184

Wholesale

Think Wholesale!

Entrepreneurs must understand the principles that govern wholesale trade, especially if you are offering a product to the public. By definition, a wholesale item is one that is purchased at cost and then sold again for a profit. Manufacturers sell goods wholesale to buyers who represent outlets, such as retail stores where the items will be sold to the public.

Manufacturers set wholesale price points for buyers based on volume. The more units you buy at wholesale, the less the per unit price. If you are the procuring agent for your company, of course you want to get the best wholesale price. Much of American manufacturing needs are now produced overseas. You need to figure additional costs on top of your wholesale item price that includes shipping fees, customs and port fees, customs brokers and local transportation.

Smaller retail outlets have to set higher prices for their wares than large so-called big-box stores. The large, mega-stores can afford to charge less because they paid less, and they are selling more items than the smaller stores.

Major wholesale suppliers display their goods at trade shows attended by buyers such as you or your procurement manager. Oftentimes you can even deal directly with the factory where the items are made and cut out the brokers or middlemen. Learn the different avenues to get your best wholesale prices.

And note, that even service providers are outsourcing their services and getting wholesale prices. For example, many accounting firms now outsource their needs to overseas companies located in India whose accountants do excellent work for a fraction of what an American accountant charges. The US accounting firm thereby saves money and can build up their profit margin. Service providers such as phone companies and tech companies do the same thing. Always think wholesale!

Withstand

The Power of Withstanding!

Entrepreneurs must develop the power to withstand adversity as early as possible. To withstand means to remain undamaged or unaffected by outside forces, to offer strong resistance or opposition to something. As an entrepreneur you have to withstand the challenges that will confront you, both external and internal. Having the ability to withstand opposing forces is imperative for you to win the game of entrepreneurship.

By withstanding, I do not mean to imply that you should take a lot of foolishness from ignorant people. Instead, I am saying that you should stand tall for what is true, or what is rightfully yours. You do this by remaining undaunted and unaffected by what people say, think, or do to stop you from doing what you set out to do. This kind of staying power allows you to continue your journey to success no matter what forces are arrayed against you.

Yes, you must take a heroic stance. Every great story has a hero who through their own devices—and oftentimes with some timely help—is able to rise above the odds that confront them. Yes, this is a tall order. Are you really up for it?

Before you decide to embark on your entrepreneurial journey, can you muster up the power within yourself to withstand anything, even in the face of serious challenges from your own team, your family, your suppliers, your customers, the weather, financial downturns, even a pandemic? Can you withstand your own inner doubts and fears?

Remember that you do have the power to be steadfast, and the resolve to withstand all challenges in business and in life. That power is derived from your pure intentions and your unreserved efforts. Through your strategic planning and your innovative skills, alongside your daily meditation, affirmative prayers and visioning, you certainly can and will develop the power to not only withstand whatever comes your way but to brilliantly prevail against the opposing forces. And the Universe will support you!

Wisdom

The Wisdom of Gaining Wisdom!

Though being an entrepreneur can seem like a wild idea to those who are not willing to take the chances you are, you must understand that underlying wisdom must be a crucial factor in your undertaking. Wisdom is defined as soundness of actions or decisions deriving from the application of experience, knowledge, insight, astuteness and good judgment; wisdom is the body of knowledge and principles that develops universally in specific areas or circumstances.

As an entrepreneur you must exercise wisdom in all of your business dealings, just as you must do in your life. You can gain wisdom from being in the company of masters, sages, elders, mentors and teachers. These wise persons can be found in every business sector and in every walk of life. By following a wise person's advice, you are able to avoid making the mistakes they have made in their ventures.

Of course, mistakes can help one gain wisdom but that is the most difficult way for one to learn. The Chinese sage Confucius said that imitation is best way to learn. Education gives you knowledge but sadly, there are many educated fools who teach because they can't do. Wisdom goes beyond just knowing things; it teaches you the best way to do things with what you know.

Once you obtain wisdom, you can execute sound judgment when challenges confront you. Every entrepreneur needs to learn to be wise. Obtain wisdom as soon as possible!

Willpower

Develop Your Willpower!

As an entrepreneur, establish and fortify your willpower. Your willpower allows everything in your consciousness to come forth and manifest in the material world. If you have strong willpower it means you have a strong personal inner force that controls where you exert your energy and where you restrain your energy. We've all heard the stories of a mom whose child is stuck under a car and through sheer willpower she is able to life a car to get her child out from under it.

You can command your negative impulses through your willpower. I have a friend who smoked 2 packs of cigarettes a day. On a business trip to Hong Kong during the hot, humid summer months, he suddenly found himself unable to breathe. He quit smoking that day and has not had an interest in cigarettes for more than 30 years—a stark example of willpower indeed if you consider how difficult it is for most smokers to quit that harmful habit.

Use willpower to control your thoughts and emotions, your words and deeds. Willpower is a mental capacity that each of us can develop. Start to develop your willpower with small things by doing something you don't like to do, or by restraining yourself from a bad habit.

Willpower is absolutely necessary to fulfill your entrepreneurial goals, as well as your evolution in becoming a beneficial presence on the planet. Once you exercise your willpower, that magnet of powerful mental energy will draw to you everything that you need and desire for your business. That's called 'The Law of Attraction.' The unseen force of willpower is the very principle that allows things that seem impossible to become possible.

And a subtle point to remember in the discussion of willpower is the concept of willingness. Once you establish your willpower, be willing and receptive to let the Universe guide you. The Universe will give you unmistakable signs that the power of your will is leading you toward the highest good. You can overcome any obstacle starting with the right willpower!

Wear

What Are You Wearing?

You have undoubtedly heard the expression: Dress for success! An entrepreneur is always mindful of what they are wearing because what you wear makes a statement about you and your company. Unfortunately, every book is judged by its cover. I am not discussing uniforms now, as we did previously. If you see a shabby, homeless person in the street, of course you are going to make a judgement about that person. If you are interviewing a candidate for a position, of course you will immediately notice and mentally record what they wore for the interview.

Your attire should be communicating your core values in business. Sure, if you are manufacturing and selling surfboards, nobody is going to be surprised if you walk into their office wearing board shorts and a Hawaiian shirt. From the top of your head to the soles of your feet, be in sync with what you want to relate to your customers and clients about yourself and your company. Your business attire may be different in different situations but you are always conscious of the visuals you are presenting to your team members, a potential investor or client.

I have a friend who owns an art gallery and is dressed every day in a nice suit or jacket with a tie, nice trousers and shoes. He dresses this way, whether he is scheduled to meet an important art collector that day or in case one walks into his gallery without an appointment. On installation day, when the gallery is closed and new art is being installed on the walls by his work crew, he is also formally dressed for two reasons; first, in case an art collector unexpectedly knocks on the closed door, and second, to let his crew know that he is still the boss even though they are busy hammering on the walls, creating dust and hanging new art pieces.

So, again, always dress for success! You have no idea who you will meet each day, and the law of attraction may even bring you that unexpected important person who you don't want to apologize to for being in your torn jeans that day. Dress up and you'll feel up!

Wages

It's More Than Just Wages!

As an entrepreneur, understand the importance of paying your team members fair wages. The federal government has established a minimum wage, which for the most part is just that—a minimum or starting salary.

Tell your employees right from the start that the company does periodic performance and salary reviews. When you find someone who you see is willing to go the extra mile when asked, or especially when they put in extra effort unasked, then note that to yourself, and to that valuable employee.

Sometimes employers forget that human capital is the most important revenue-producing resource they have and they don't reward their team enough through praise or a raise. Employees have said in surveys over and over again that wages are important to their work effort but what really motivates them is seeing their job as something of further value to themselves and society. Entrepreneurs oftentimes get caught up in the larger issues at their company and they tend overlook a great employee or just take for granted their contribution. Why does a person like that then leave your company? It's not just the wages.

Pay attention to all your employees, and assess their worth in terms of wages or other benefits. If you can't pay the wages a really experienced or valuable employee deserves, especially at the beginning of your entrepreneurial venture, figure out other compensation to offer them such as profit-sharing. Employee profit-sharing is a great workforce motivator, and produces more revenue.

Let your outstanding team members know how much they are appreciated and when the time is right, see what you can do to increase wages as a reward, or find another creative way to keep them happy at your company.

X

X-Ray

Use Your X-Ray Vision!

Being an entrepreneur, consider making what I call a "business x-ray." Just like a medical x-ray provides an image of what the naked eye cannot see, a business x-ray examines the internal and external parts, movements, and practices of your enterprise. This is a special sort of insight that gives you a sort of psychic view into your business endeavors, which can prevent you from making dumb decisions or moves.

No, this is not the woowoo part of my teachings. Sometimes you have to completely empty your mind to get clarity about a complex situation. Once you get to the point of internal calmness and spaciousness, your third eye can open up and you can look at and through all the elements presented to you in that situation. You will see things that you could not see before because your ordinary vision, using your eye and your mind's ordinary reasoning, have not seen in the heat of the moment.

As my pastor says, "Are you describing what you see, or seeing what you describe?" Too often our mind interprets what we see based on our past experiences or prejudices. When we clear out the filters, we see more clearly what is really in front of us in both life and business.

Remember to activate your x-ray vision when challenges start to overwhelm you. You'll find this extra power within you will help you to regain composure and confidence, putting you back in the driver's seat on the road to abundance, prosperity and fulfillment of your personal and business goals.

Y

Yearn

Know Your Yearnings!

Entrepreneurs must have a deep yearning. A yearning is an intense feeling of longing for something. To any individual who seeks to be in their own business, I suggest that you select an enterprise that you deeply yearn to experience, that matches your deepest soulful yearnings. Remember that the soul always seeks to be reunited with its Creator, always longs to be close to its Source.

Yearning for a business solely to make money will eventually lead you to misery. I have had several businesses that made money but once I was fully invested, I couldn't wait to find a way out of the misery that came from seeking only to make a profit. I realized that I had put my well-being—physically, emotionally, mentally and spiritually—in the hands of my misguided business yearnings. I had completely forgotten about my own initial soul's yearning for a happy, fulfilling and balanced life. The businesses that made me nearly crazy were my night club and my casino, both of which attracted some very unsavory individuals who I quickly realized that I did not want to associate myself with on a day-to-day basis.

Finally, a deep yearning arose within me to engage in a business where I would be with healthy individuals on a daily basis, performing a meaningful service or offering a great product, and where I could feel peace and contentment within myself. I finally sold out of my dark enterprise at a modest profit. However, the primary reward for me was to escape from a place that was not in alignment with my true Self.

So, I say to you, when you start your entrepreneurial endeavors be certain of what your deepest longing really is before you expend the years, money and energy that you will have to devote to your business. You want to wake up every day saying *Yes!* to your commitment to do your best and be proud of what you are doing based on the meaningful yearnings you experienced at the start of your career. Being in touch with those yearnings always will ensure a fruitful, ever-expanding enterprise for you, your team, family and community.

Yield

The Art of the Yield

Entrepreneurs understand how to get their product or service to yield. Yield has meanings that seem quite different: an amount or rate of return, to give way, or to provide. Examples: (1) The yield of the recipe was twelve brownies, (2) the driver at the left side of a 4-way stop sign yields to the driver on the right side, or (3) the rate of return on a bond yields an interest rate of 2%, or gives an investor $2.00 for every $100 invested.

Calculate well what the yield will be from the sum of your energies—your physical, mental, emotional, spiritual and financial energies. This means that that you need to know not only your financial investments and returns but how to best allocate all your various resources for the greatest yield on your state of happiness, as well as that of your team, your family and your community.

Each of your plans, decisions and actions must yield the greatest return possible for your entrepreneurial enterprise to succeed. How can you motivate your employees in order to harvest the maximum yield from their efforts? Know when it's time to pause and yield to your market's demands or conditions. When and how is it best to yield to your suppliers and your customers? Understanding the principles of yield is a very subtle tool in your toolbox to success.

The Japanese martial art of aikido is predicated on the principle of yielding to your opponent's energy. So, if an assailant is rushing at you with a knife, unlike in karate where you kick them, in aikido you grab the assailant's wrist as they close in on you and using their own momentum, you simply guide their body, through their wrist, down to the floor. Women are especially adept at aikido because they have been taught culturally from an early age to yield.

Contemplate the concepts behind the word yield and you will develop a deft skill to use in your internal business organization dealings, as well as acquiring a subtle edge on your competition.

Z

Zenith

There is None!

A true entrepreneur knows there is never a zenith to their career. The word zenith is derived from Medieval Latin; literally, "the way over the head." In astronomy, it is the point in the sky directly overhead. Figuratively, we understand the zenith to be an ultimate experiential place in our lives. Why I say that the true entrepreneur knows there is never a zenith in their career is because they never stop striving for the Infinite to which there is no zenith.

During your entrepreneurial career you will certainly reach some heights that are worthy to note and to celebrate. But, one never rests on one's laurels, which were the victor's crown in ancient Greek Olympics.

Understanding the wisdom teaching of impermanence, of course you can rejoice and indulge a bit when you overcome some seemingly impossible obstacle and reach an outstanding achievement. But, as any military leader will tell you, when you achieve a victory, keep going with that momentum. I'm not saying you should keep going till you drop from exhaustion.

Sure, there will come a day to sell out or to hand the reigns of your successful enterprise to someone younger who has more energy and newer ideas. But think of any famous scientist, for example. They may discover an important cure—even win a Nobel Prize—but they never lose their interest in research and study to discover the next big thing.

Continue to see "the way over your head" as you move from zenith to zenith in your business and personal life. A phenomenal life of never-ending riches, abundance, prosperity, and joy awaits the entrepreneur who understands the Infinite and ever-expanding Universe that has no beginning nor end, no nadir nor zenith. This is what you can expect as a true *entrepreneur*!

Made in the USA
San Bernardino, CA
08 June 2020